Meditative Mandalas

Color Me Stress Free

COLORING BOOK FOR ADULTS

BOOK TWO IN THE SERIES

Cathy Stucker

Special Interests Publishing
Sugar Land, Texas

Published by
Special Interests Publishing
Sugar Land, Texas, USA

http://SIPub.com/

The image on the cover can be found on page 13.

Some image elements herein are used under license from Shutterstock and Ingimage.

First edition published in March, 2016.

Printed in the U.S.

ISBN 978-1-888983-35-7

One of the things I love about coloring is that there are no rules!

You can stay within the lines—or not.

You can use realistic colors—or create a fantasy world.

You can color each image in the order it appears in the book, or you can skip around and color the one that appeals to you at this moment.

Coloring is about having fun and letting your worries fade away.

Grab your pens, pencils, markers, paint or whatever you love to color with, choose your favorite picture and just start coloring.

You may want to put a blank sheet of paper behind the picture you are coloring to protect the next picture from color bleeding through or impressions from the pressure used on the pen or pencil.

Want more to color? There are several more books coming soon in the Color Me Stress Free series. **Visit our Facebook page to learn how you can get FREE printable coloring pages.**

http://Facebook.com/ColorMeStressFree

Love what you have created? Share it with us and we will share it with other coloring fans.

Have any comments about this book or ideas for future books? Email me at my personal email address: cathy@idealady.com. I want to hear from you!

Happy Coloring!

Cathy

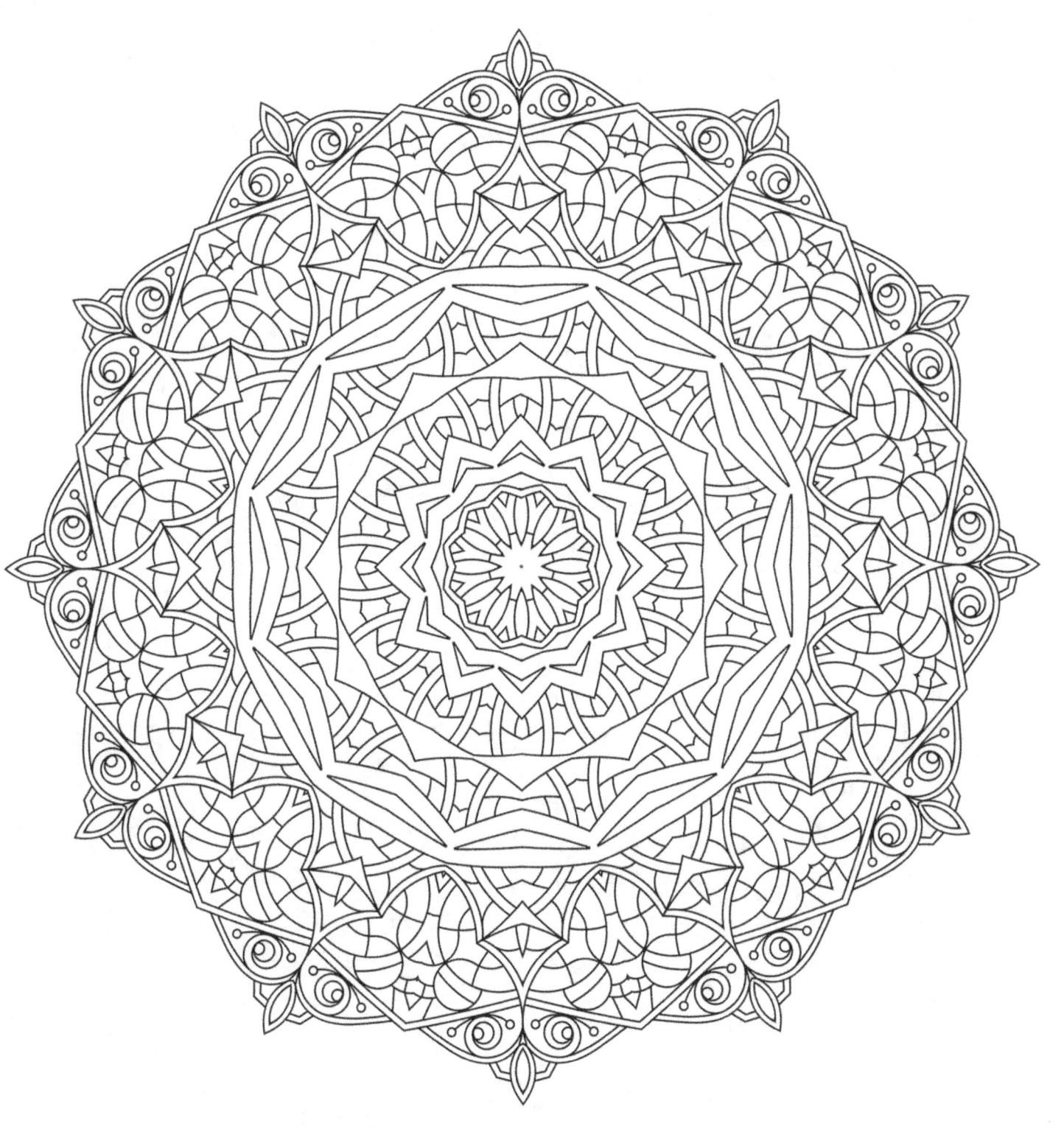

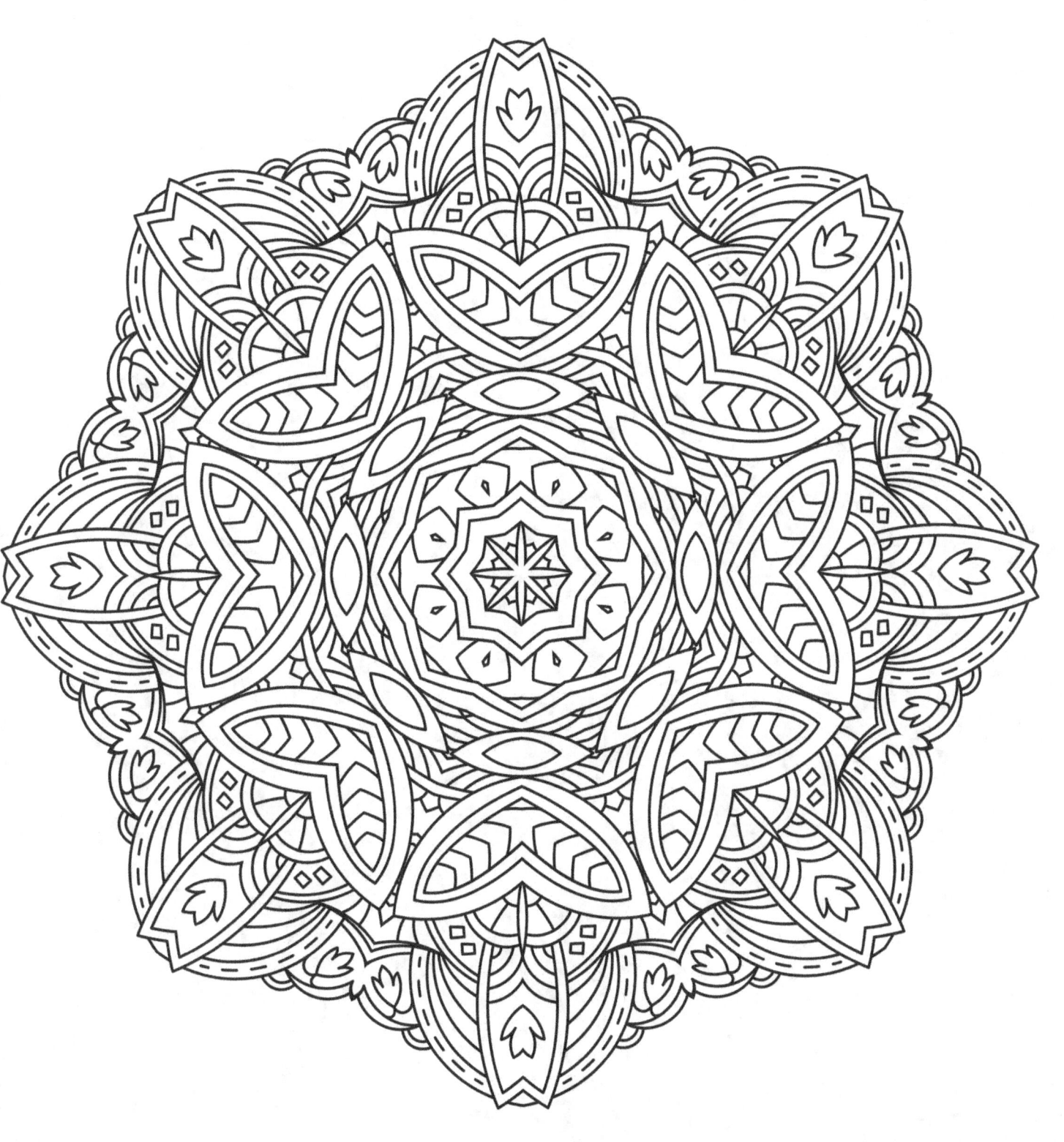

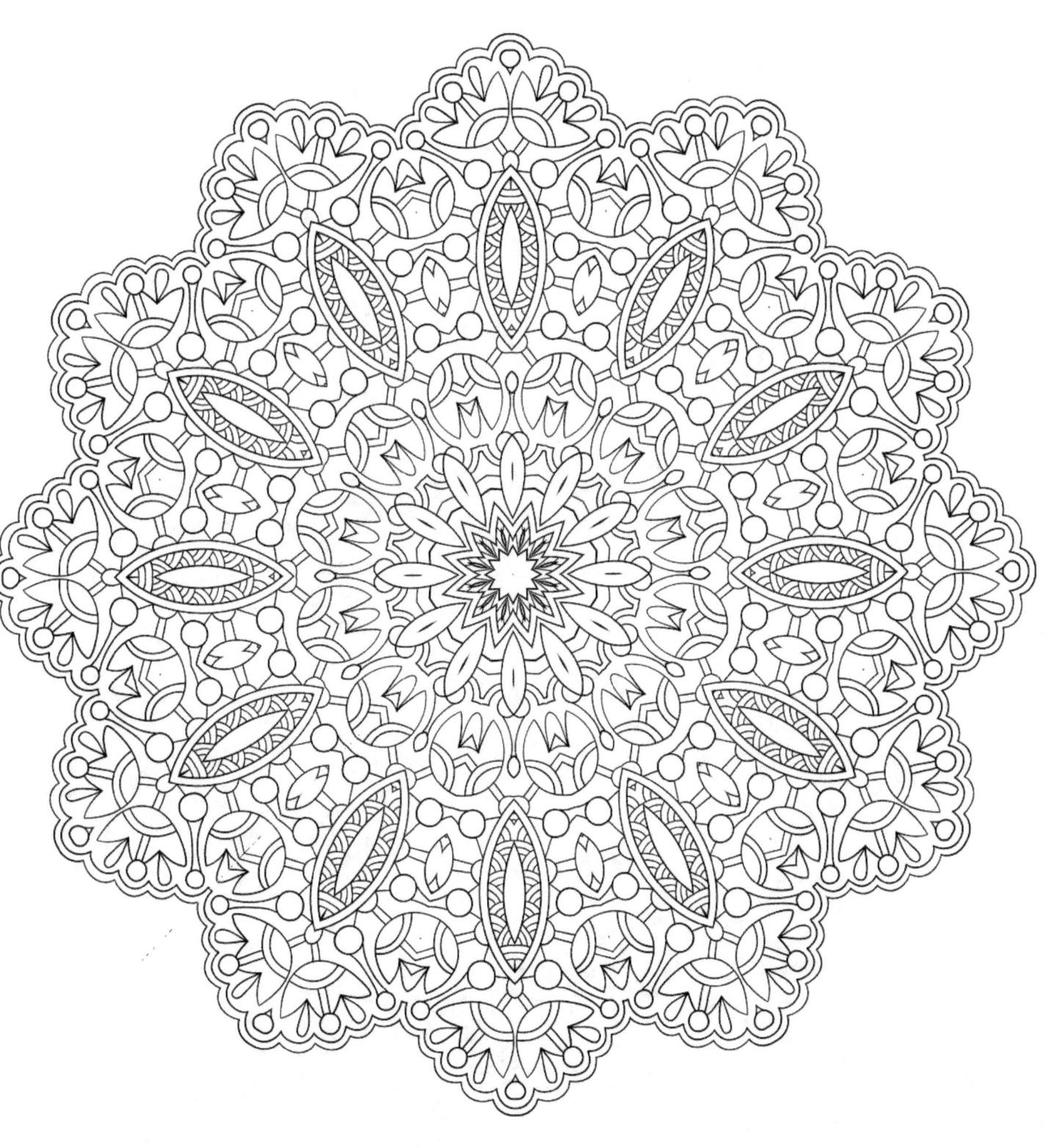

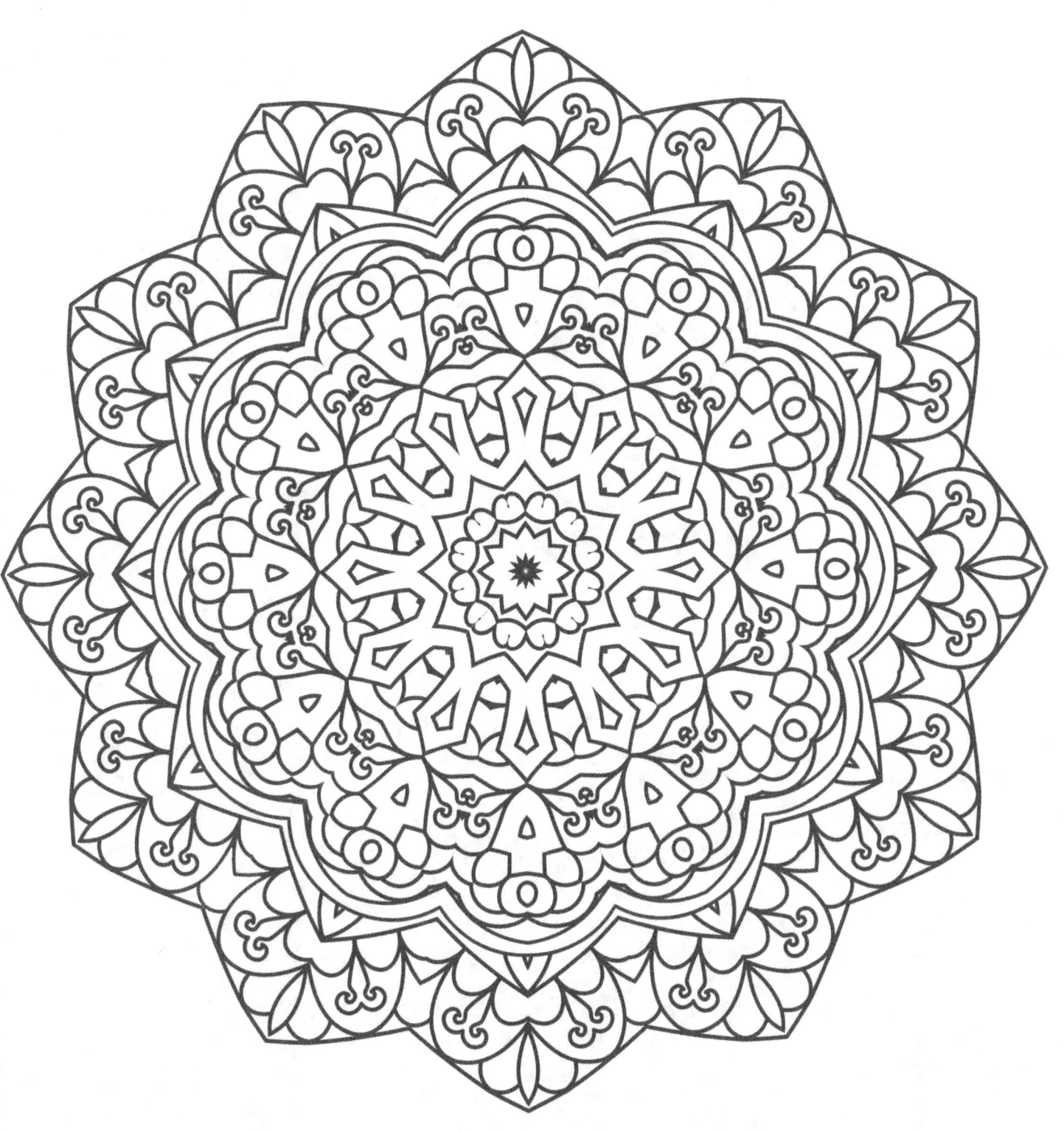

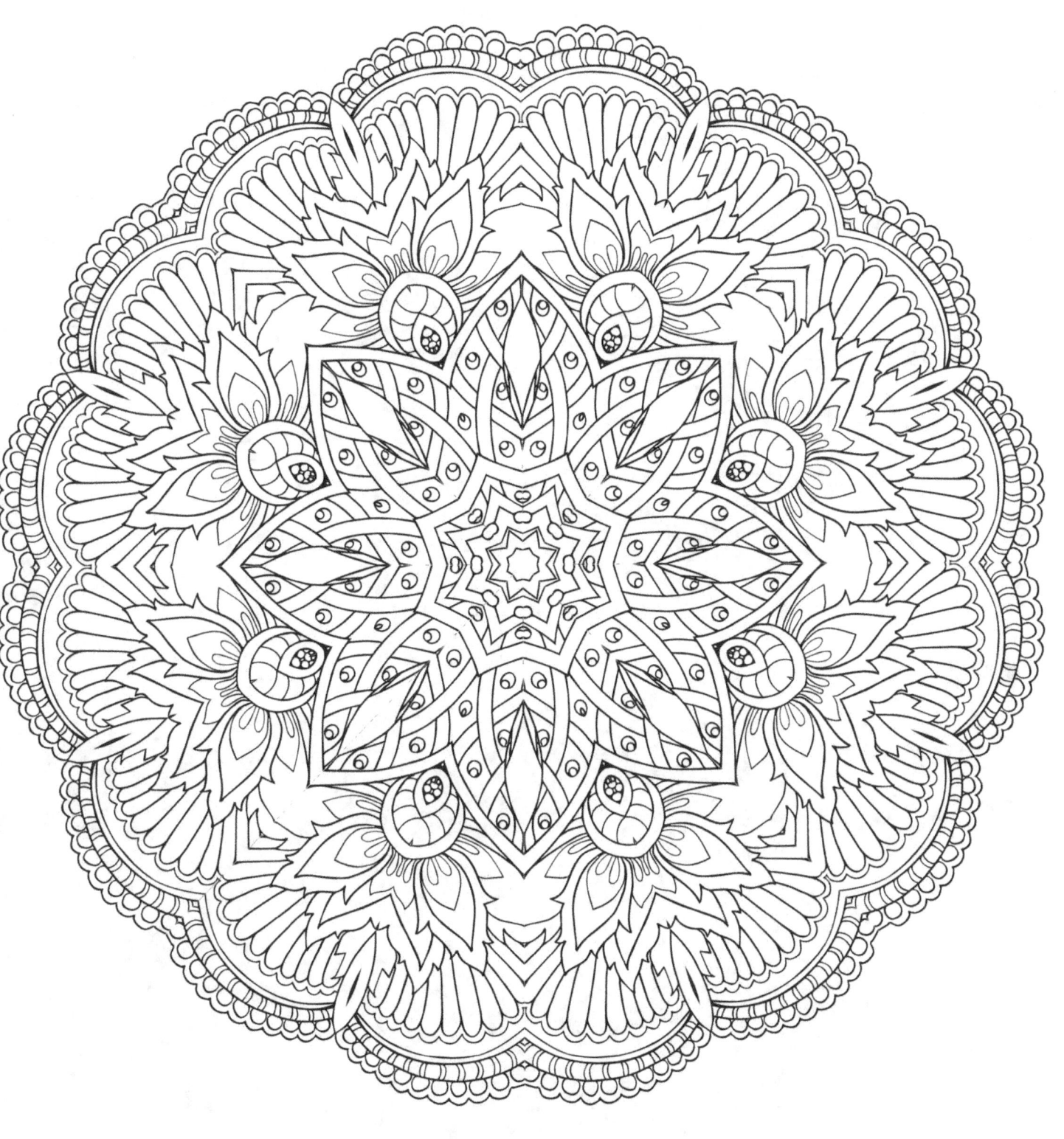

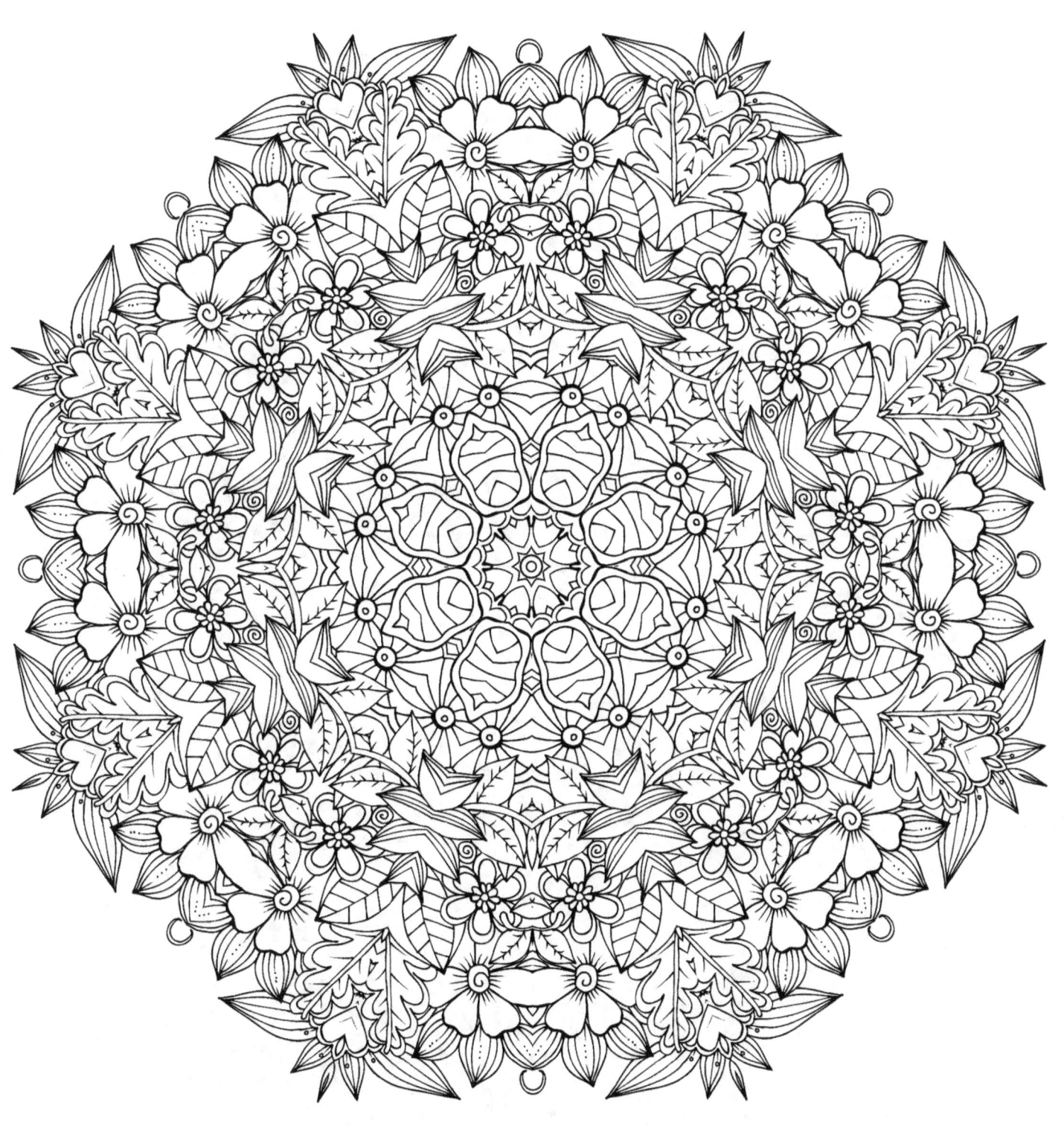

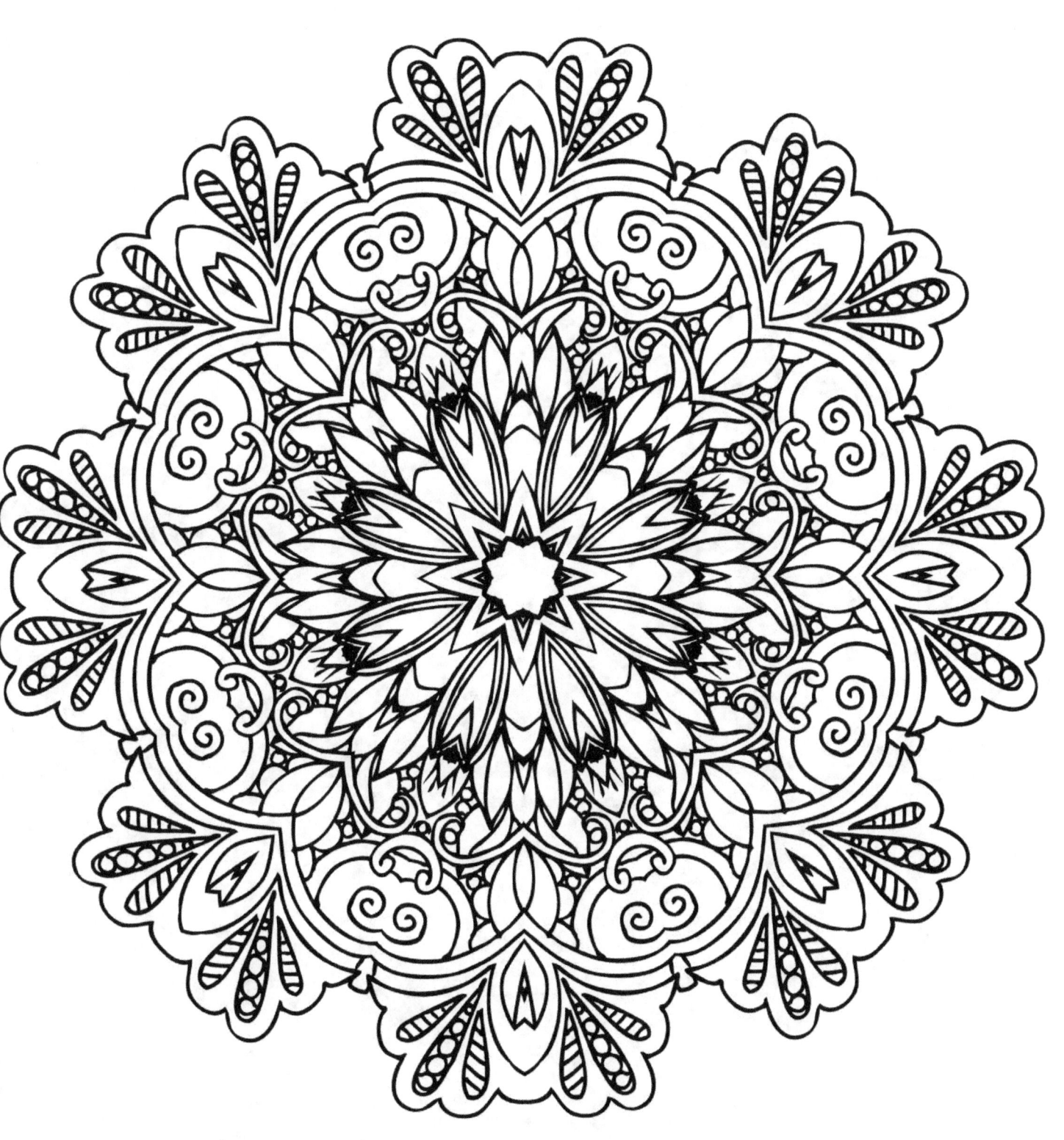

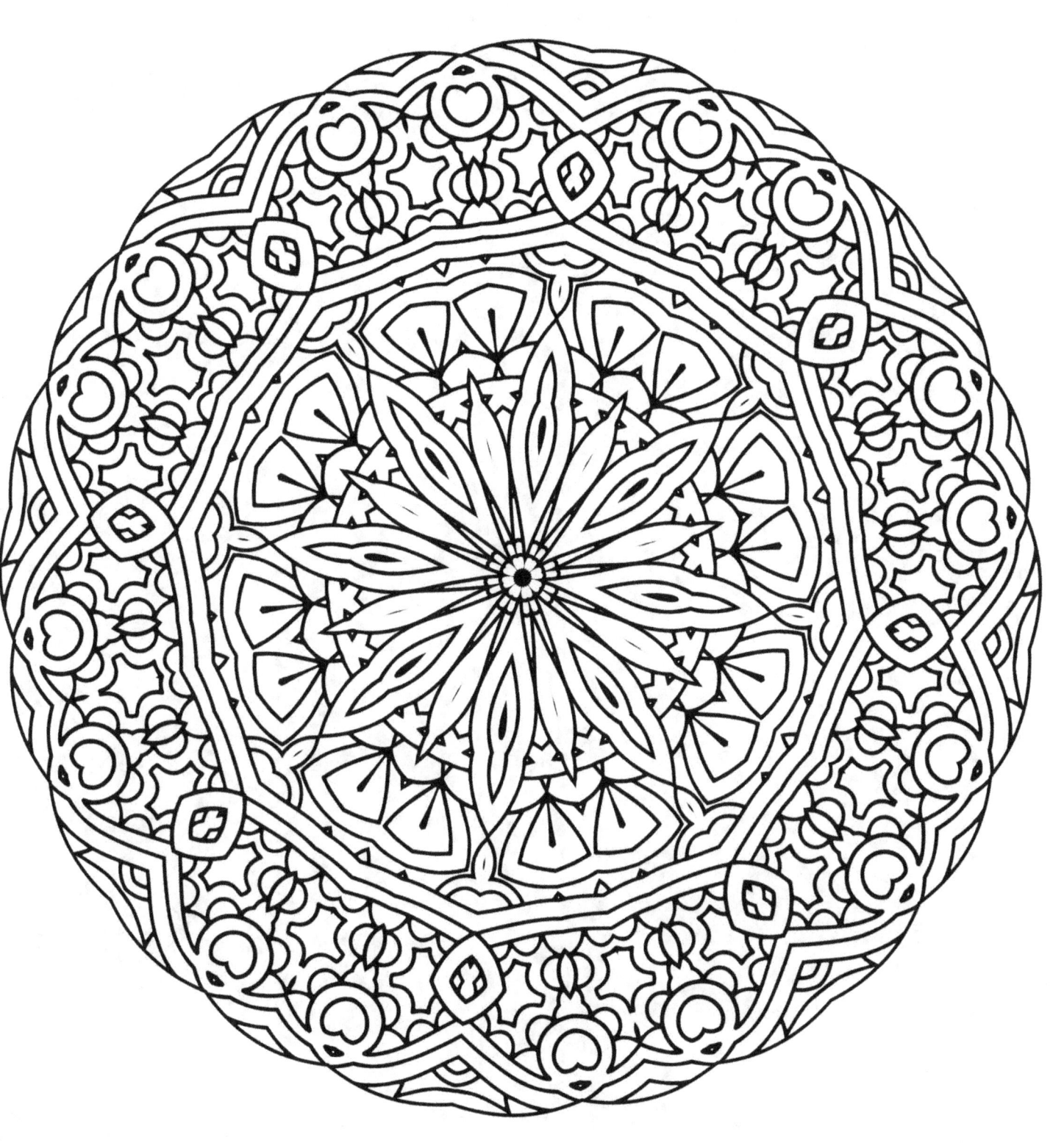

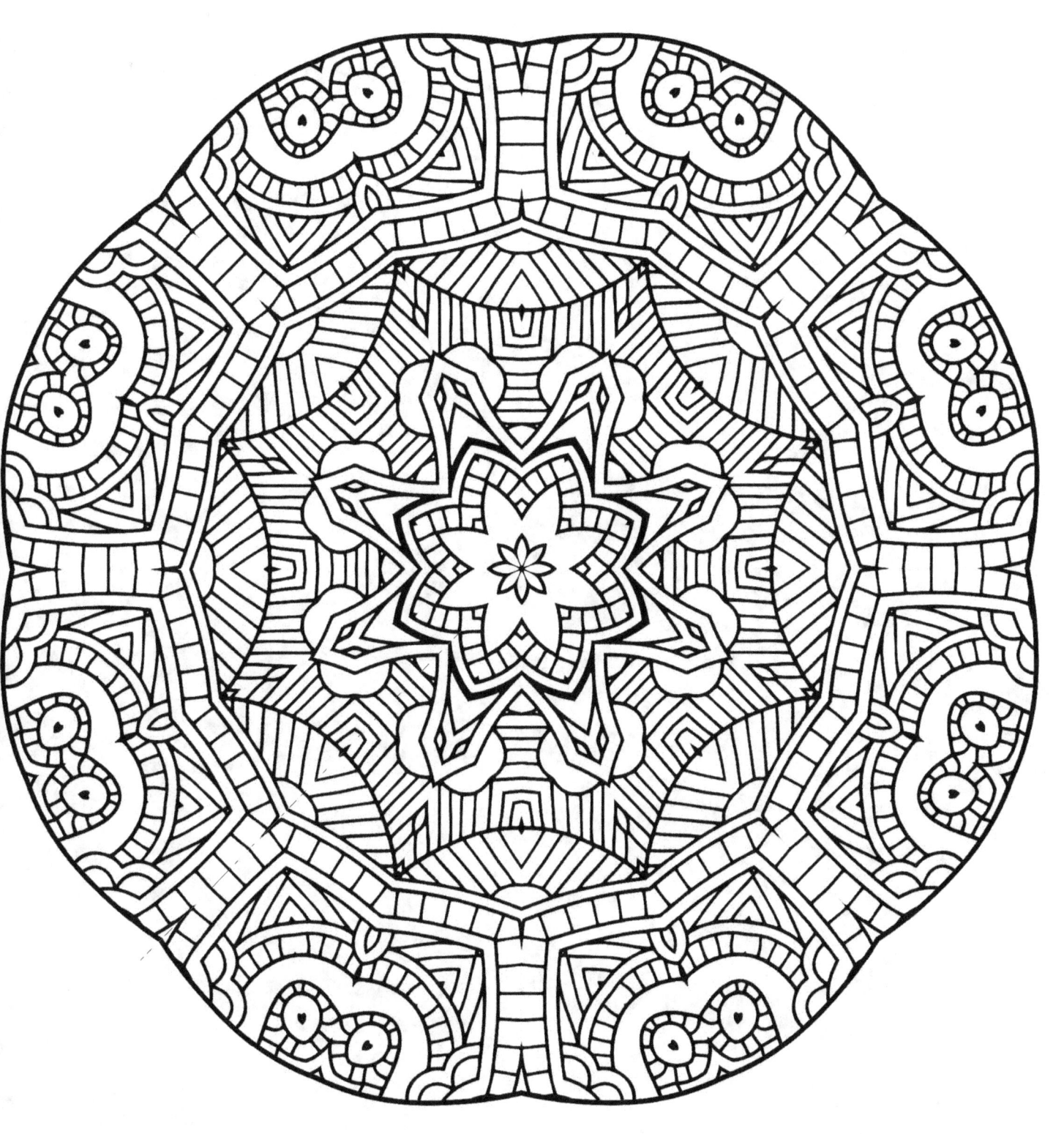

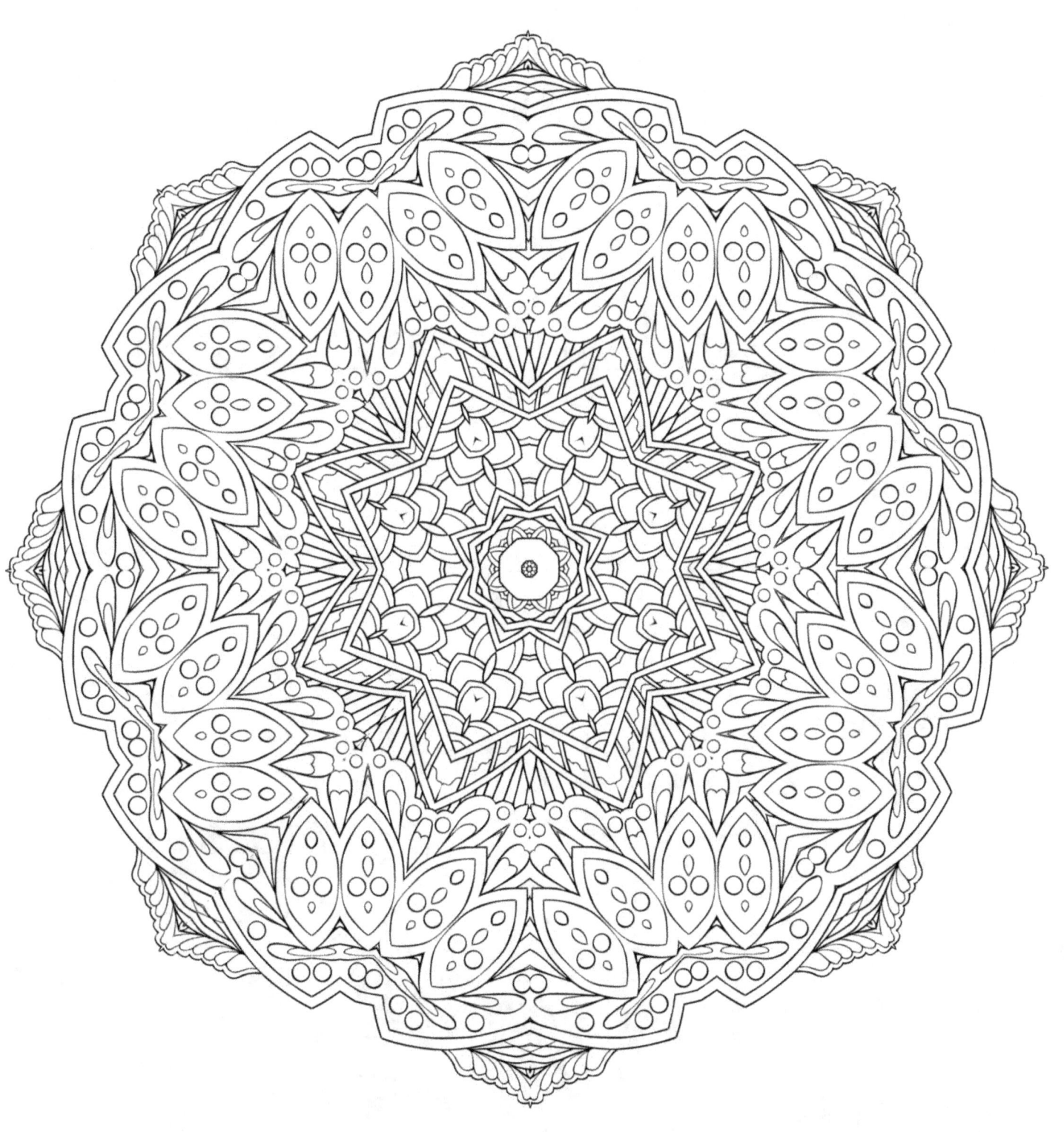

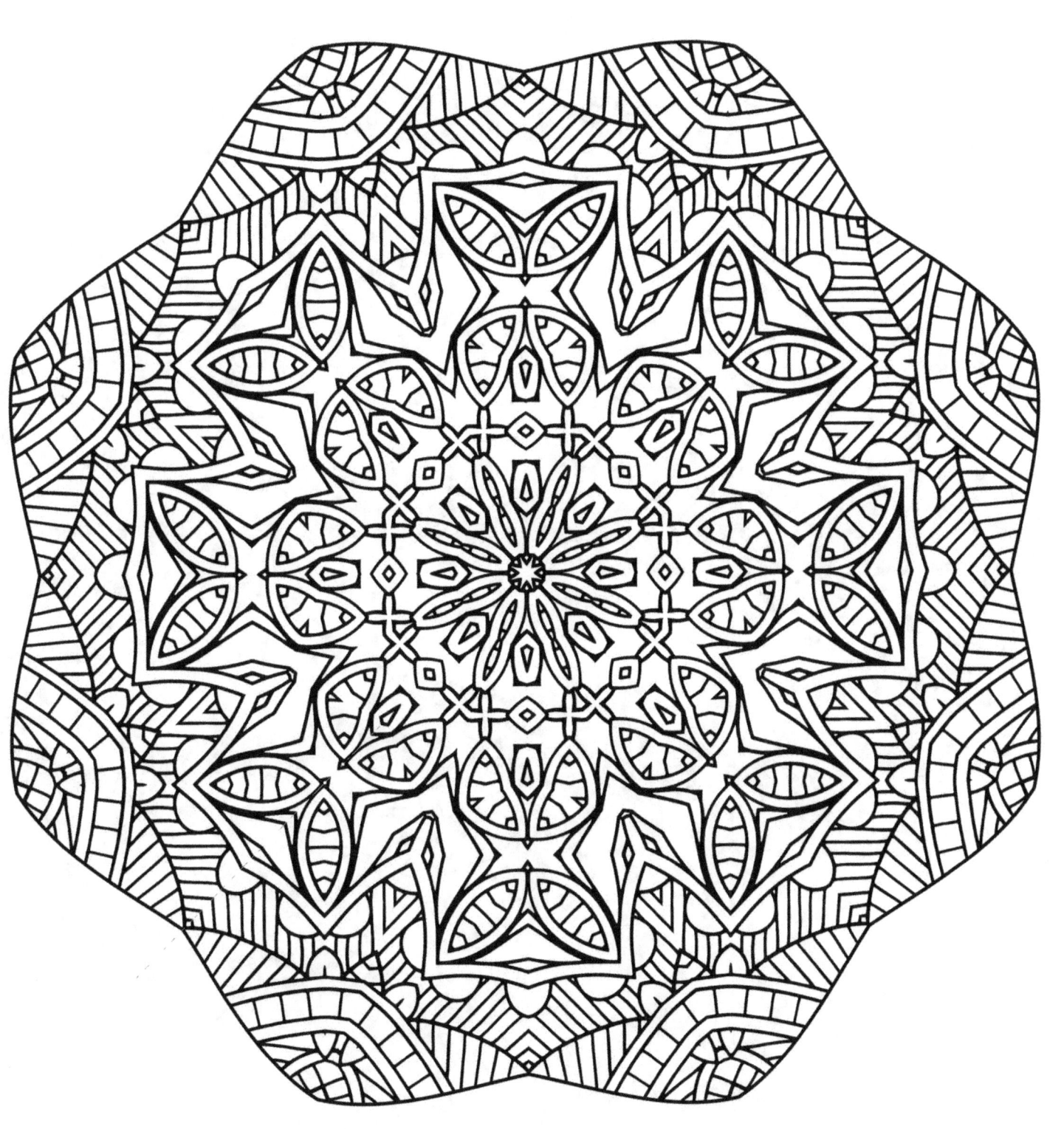

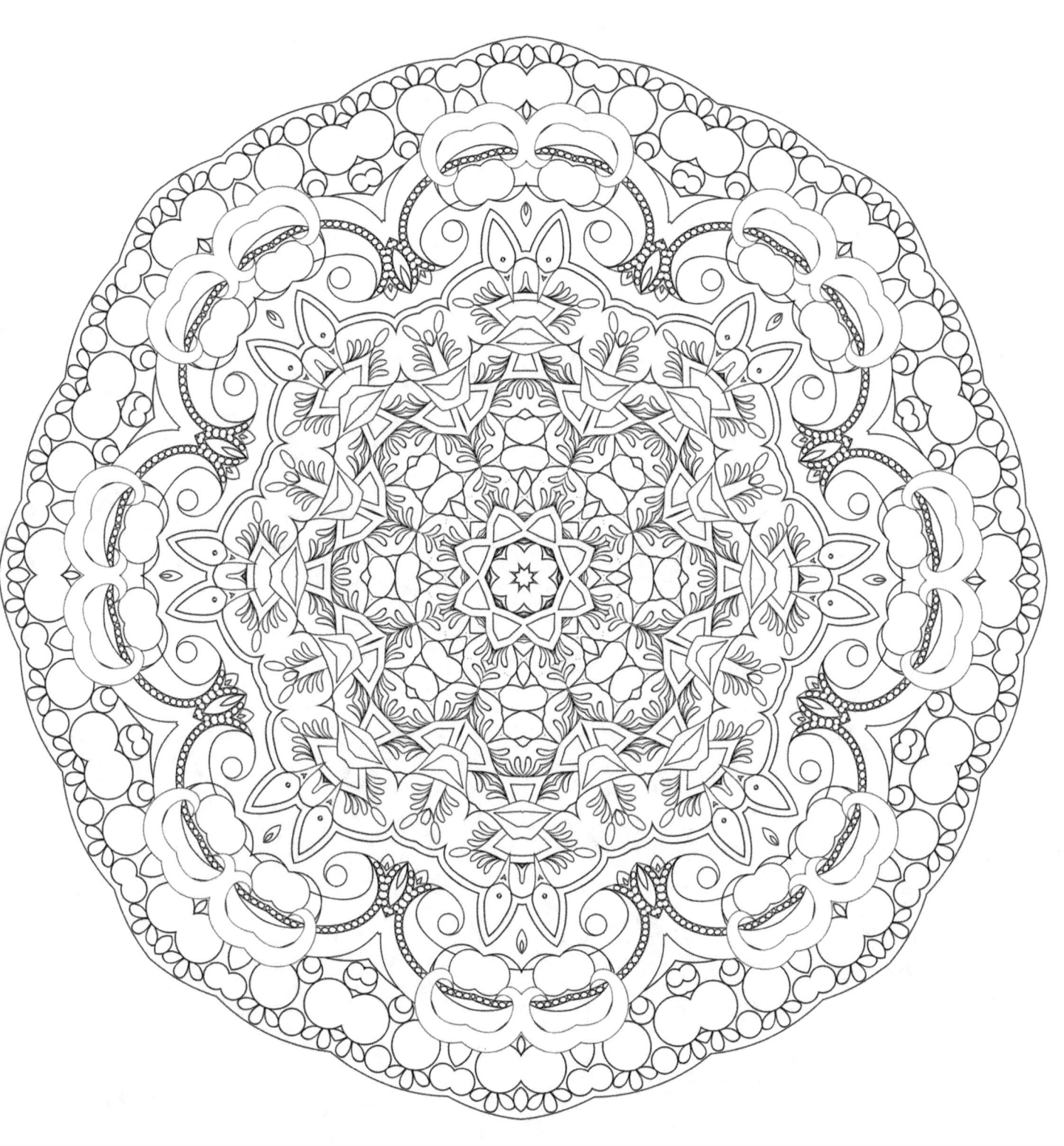

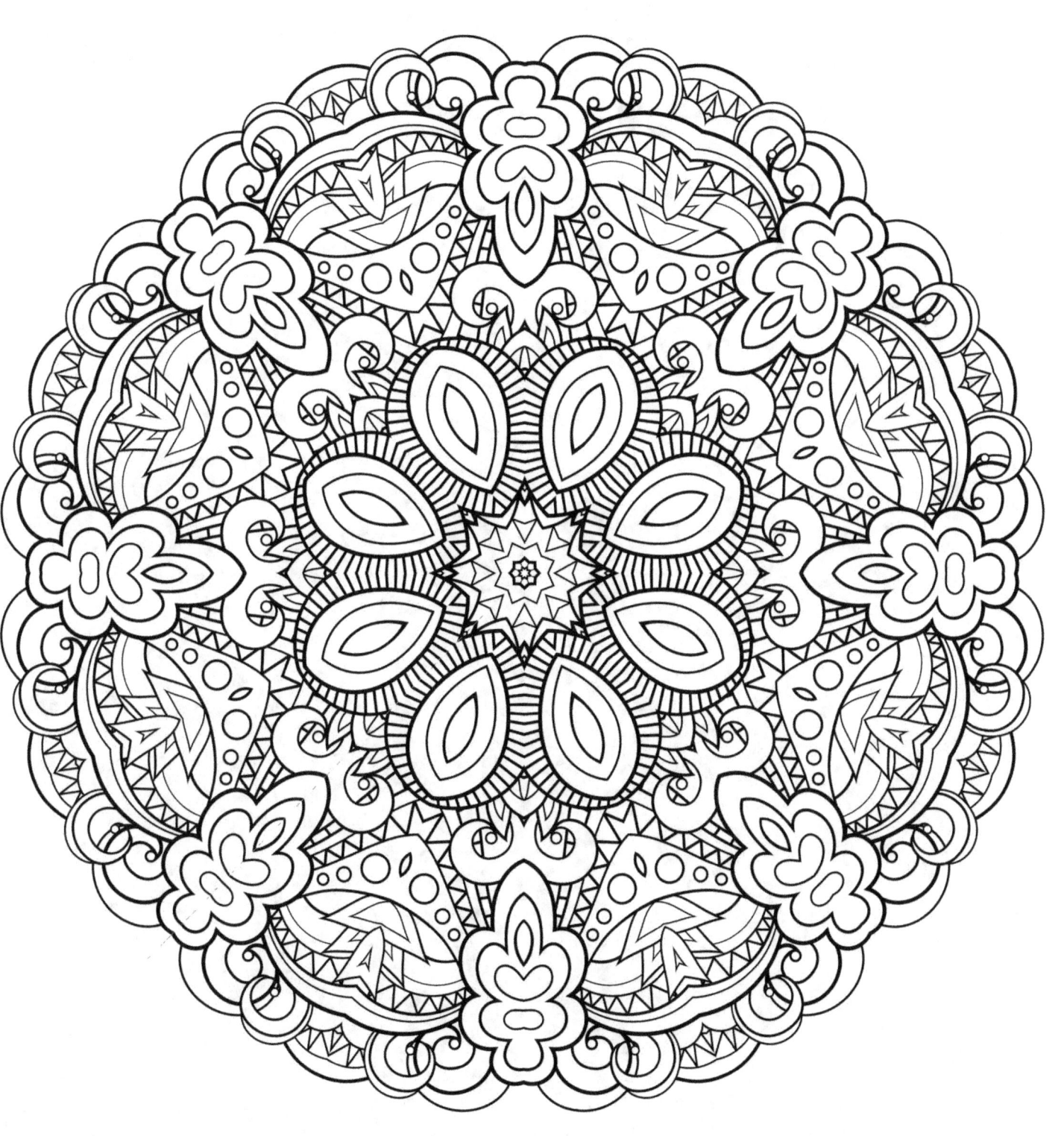

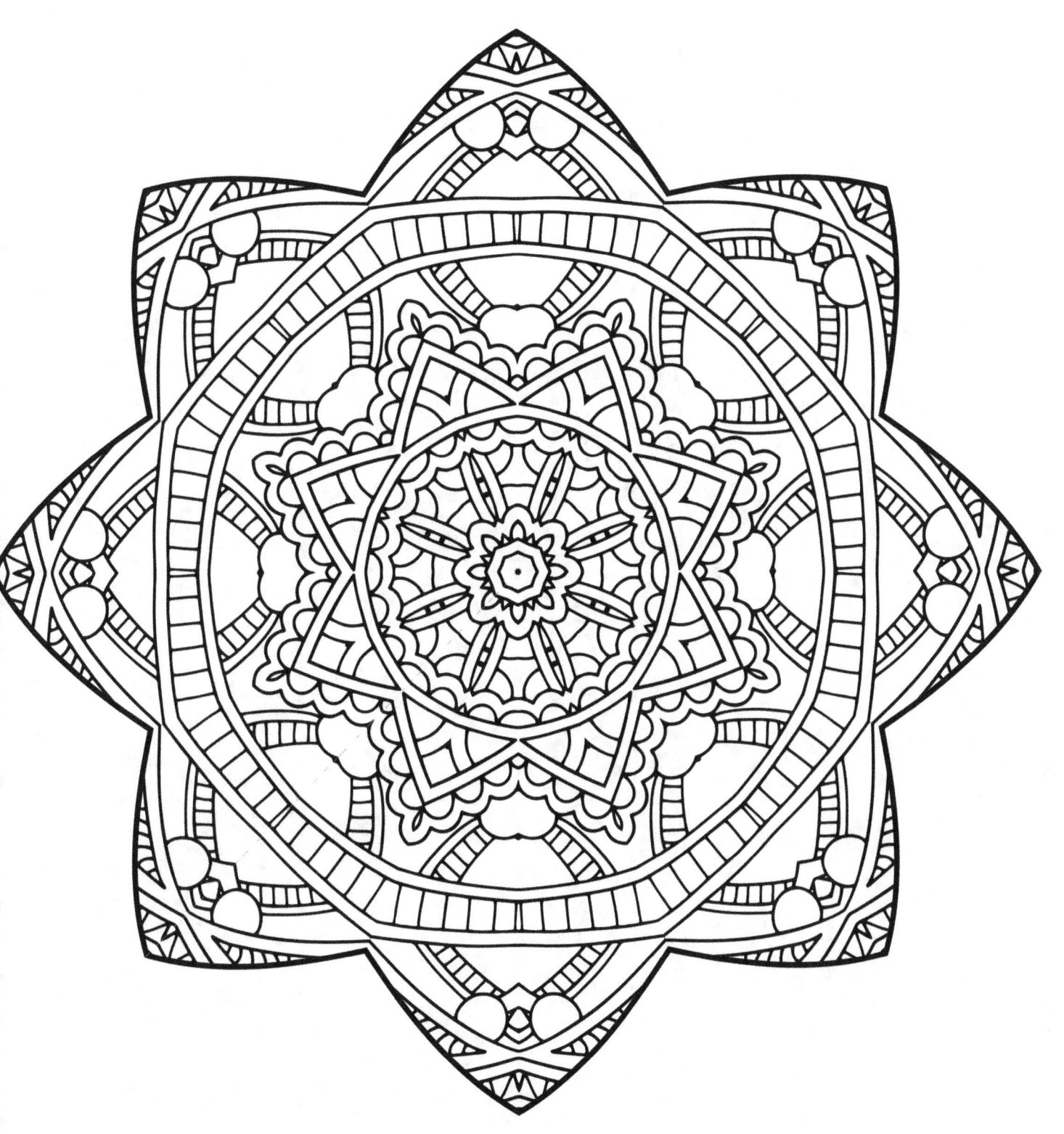

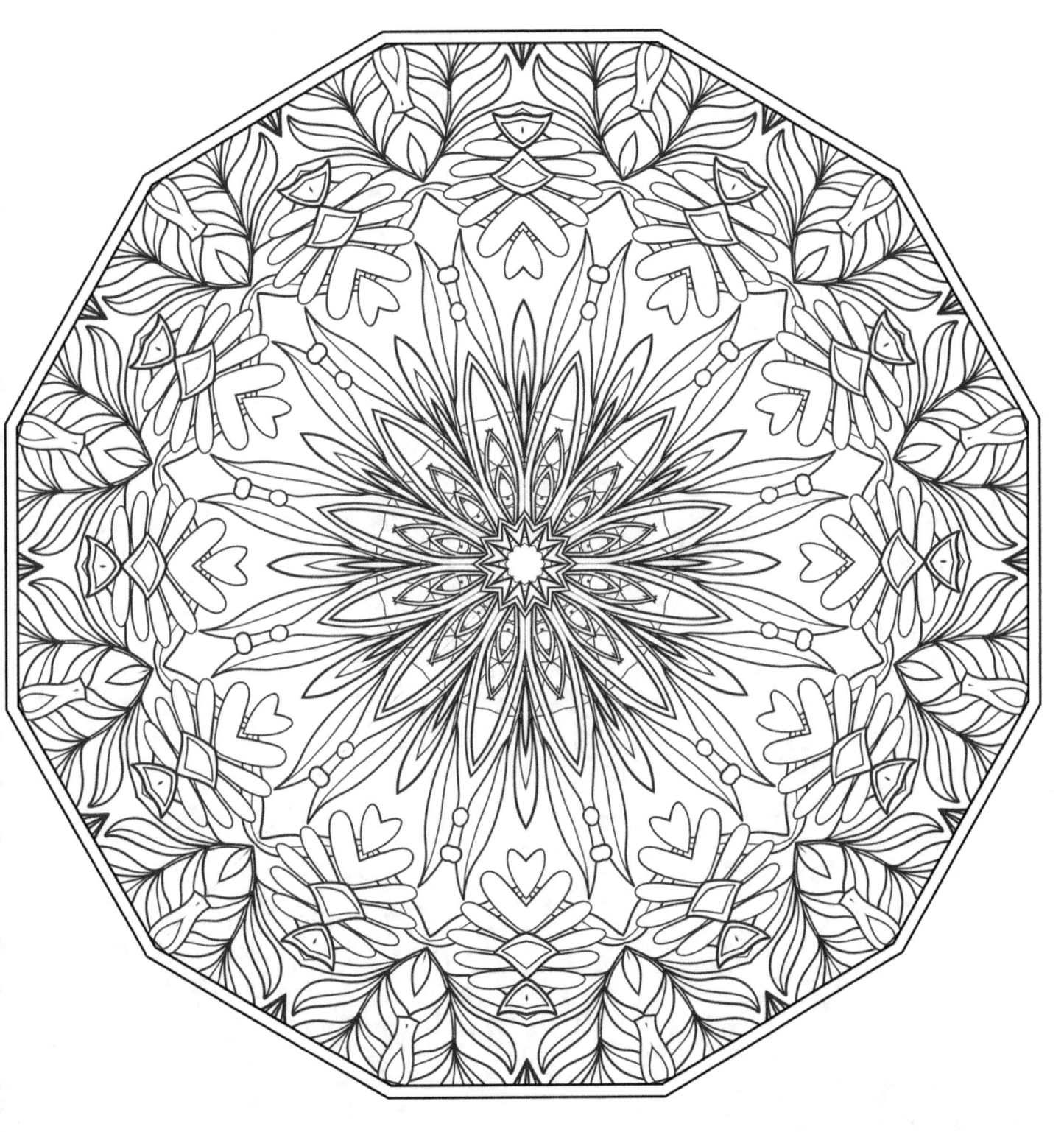

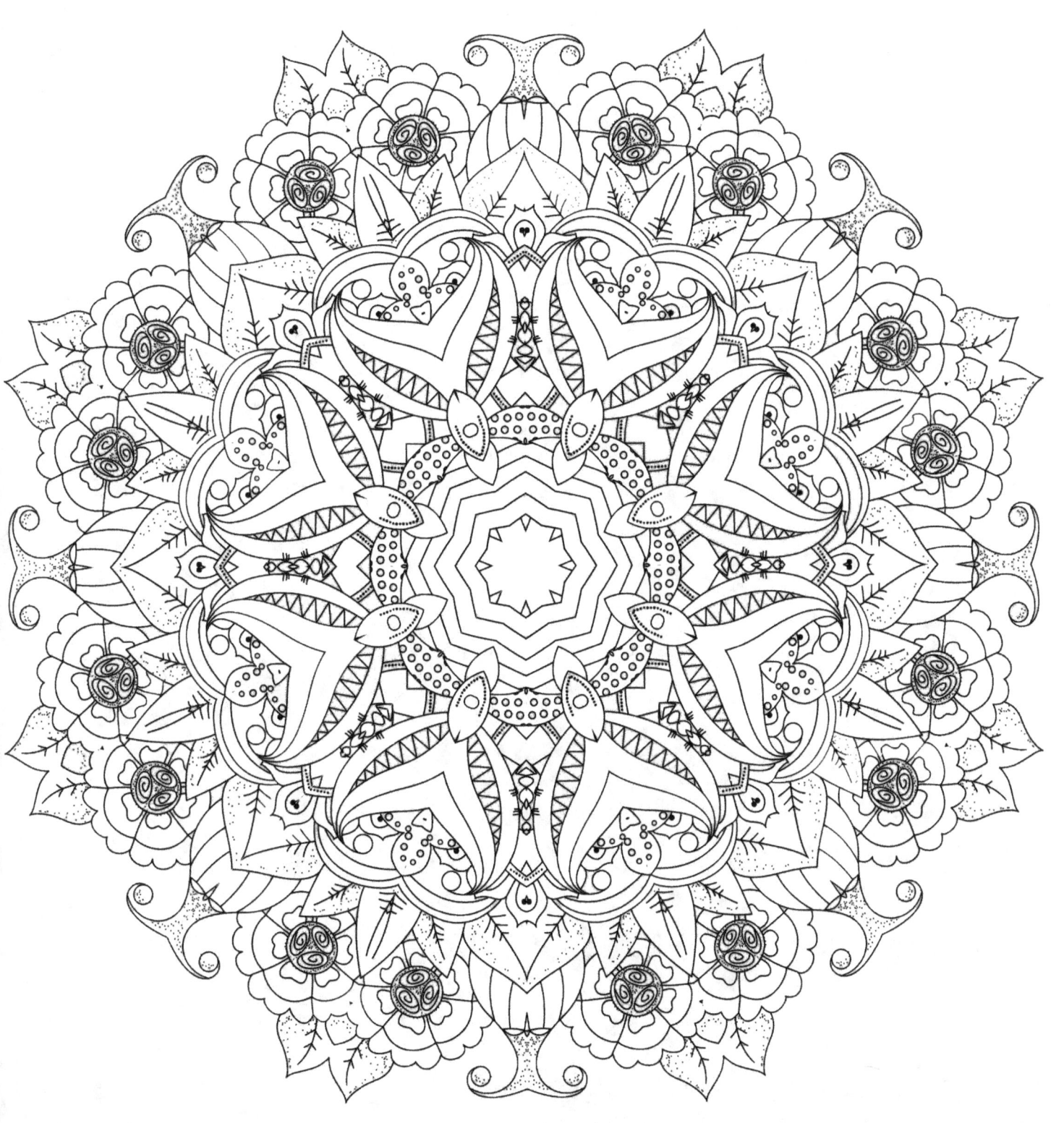

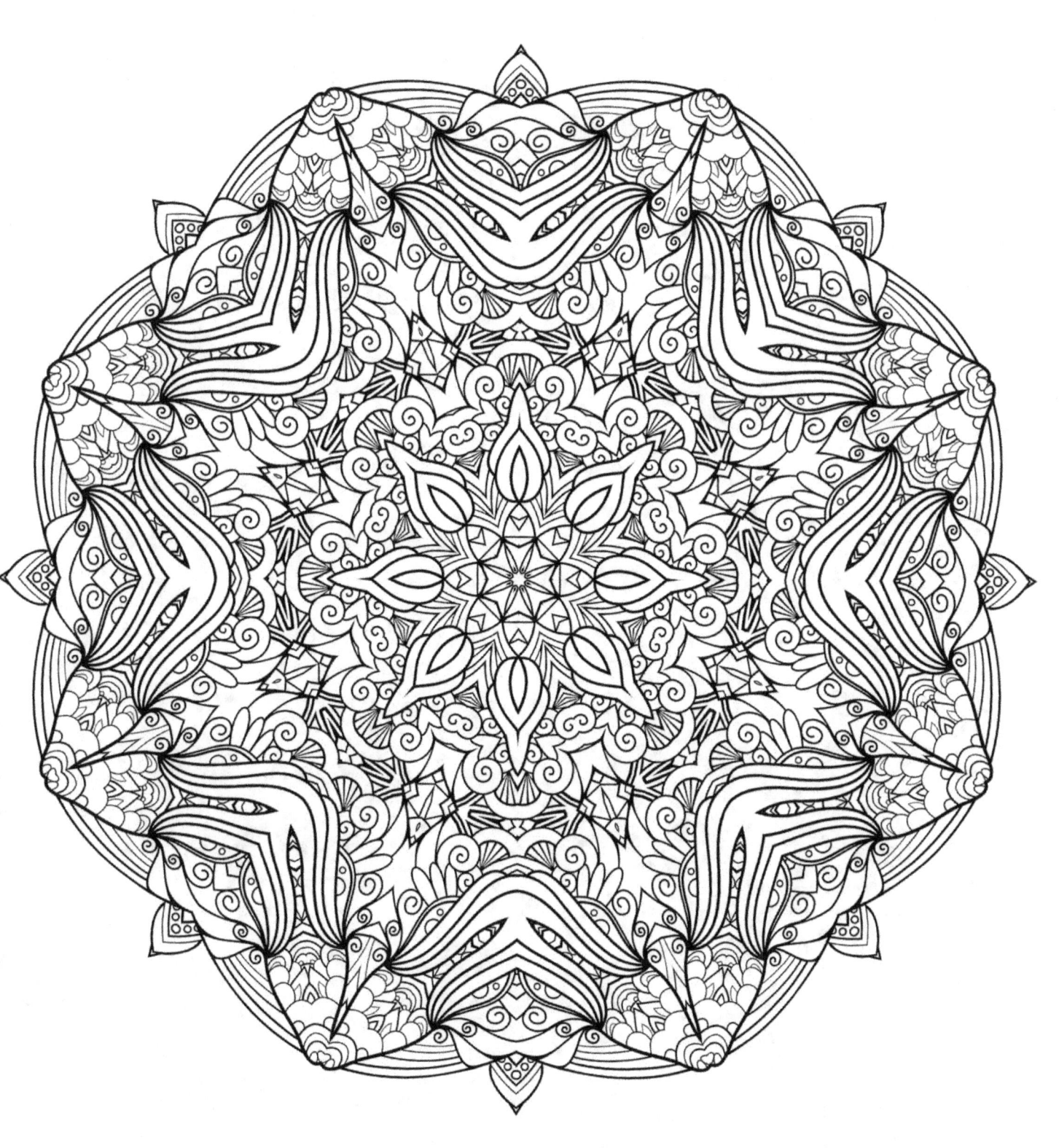

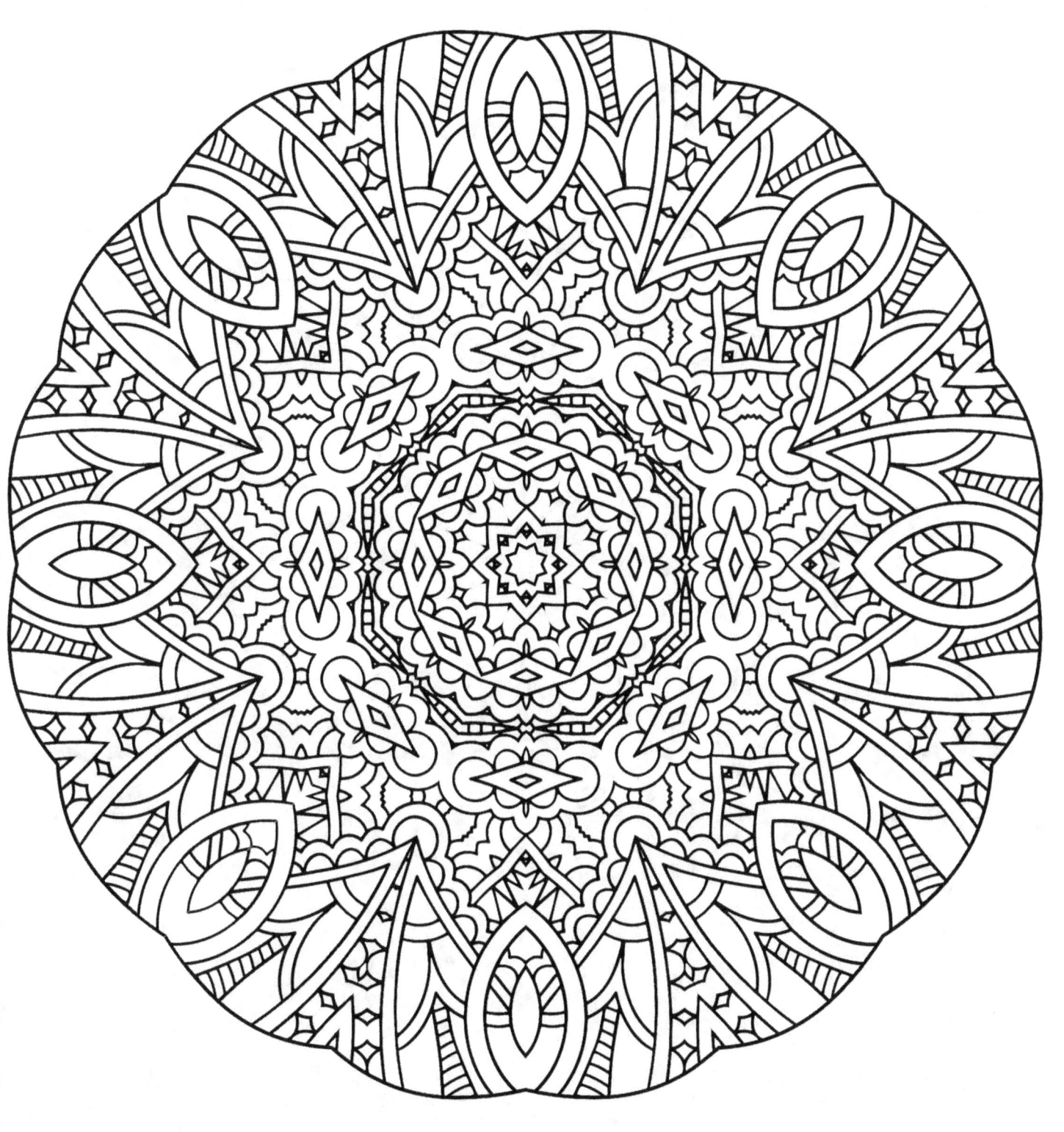

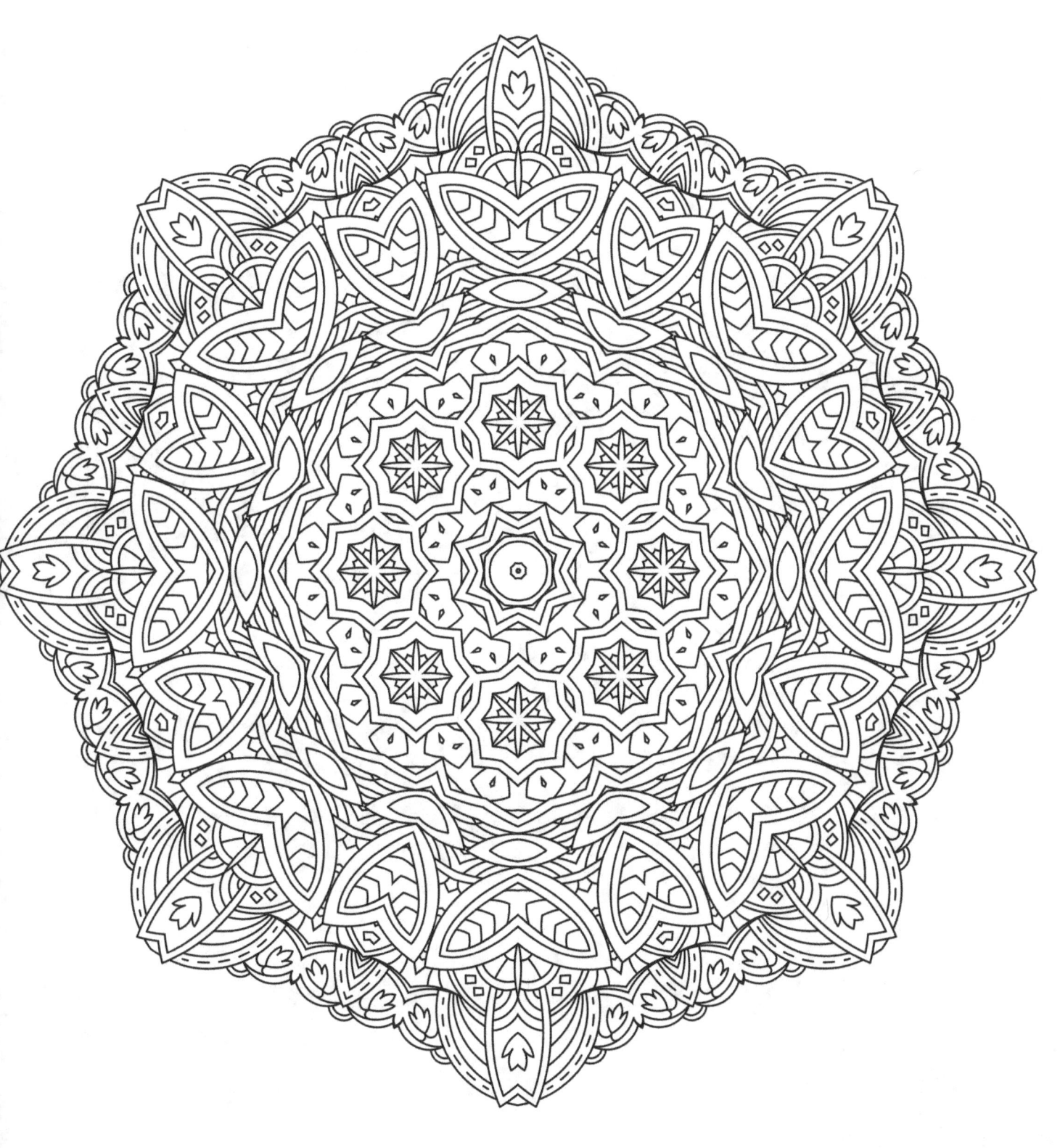

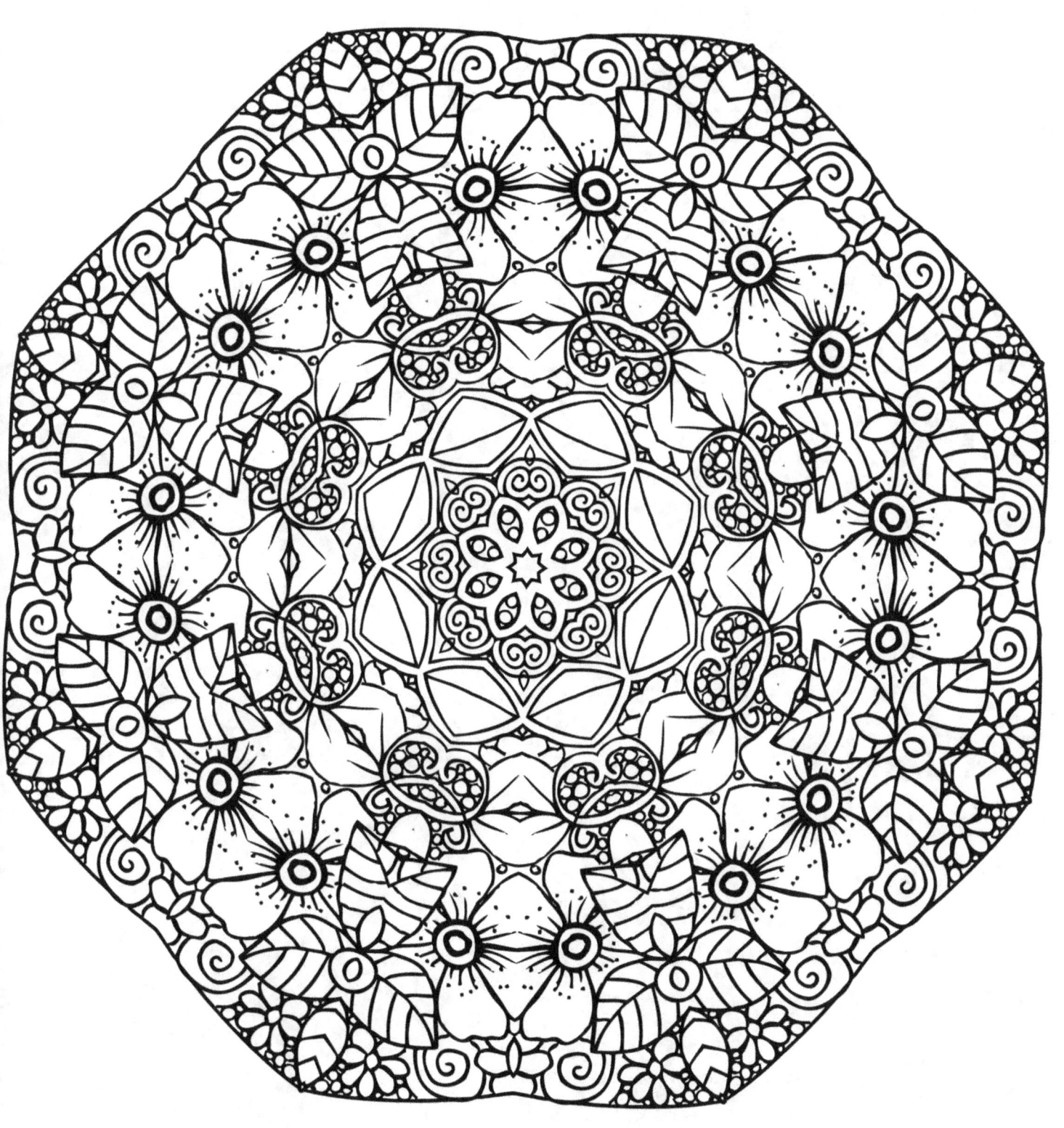

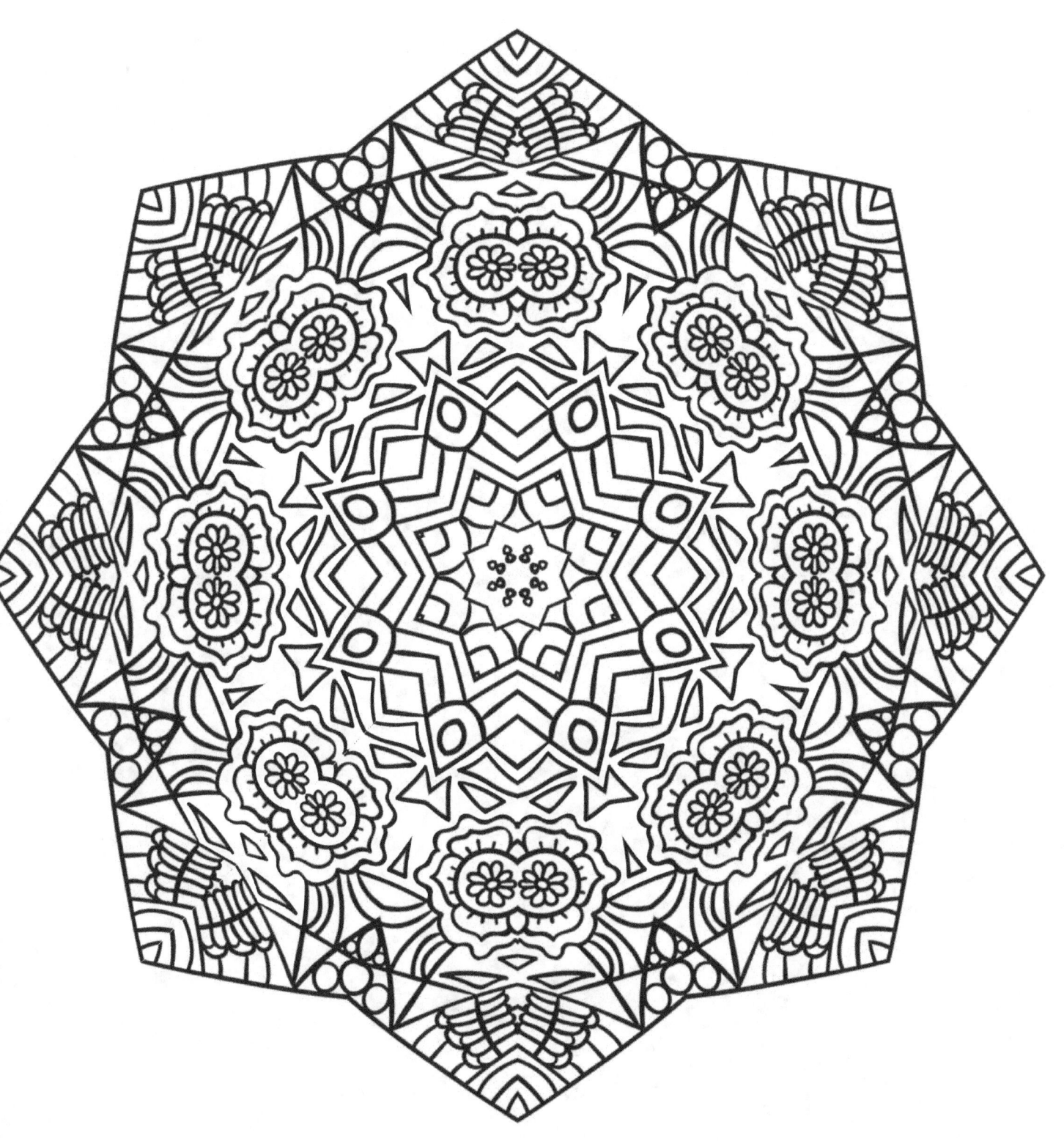

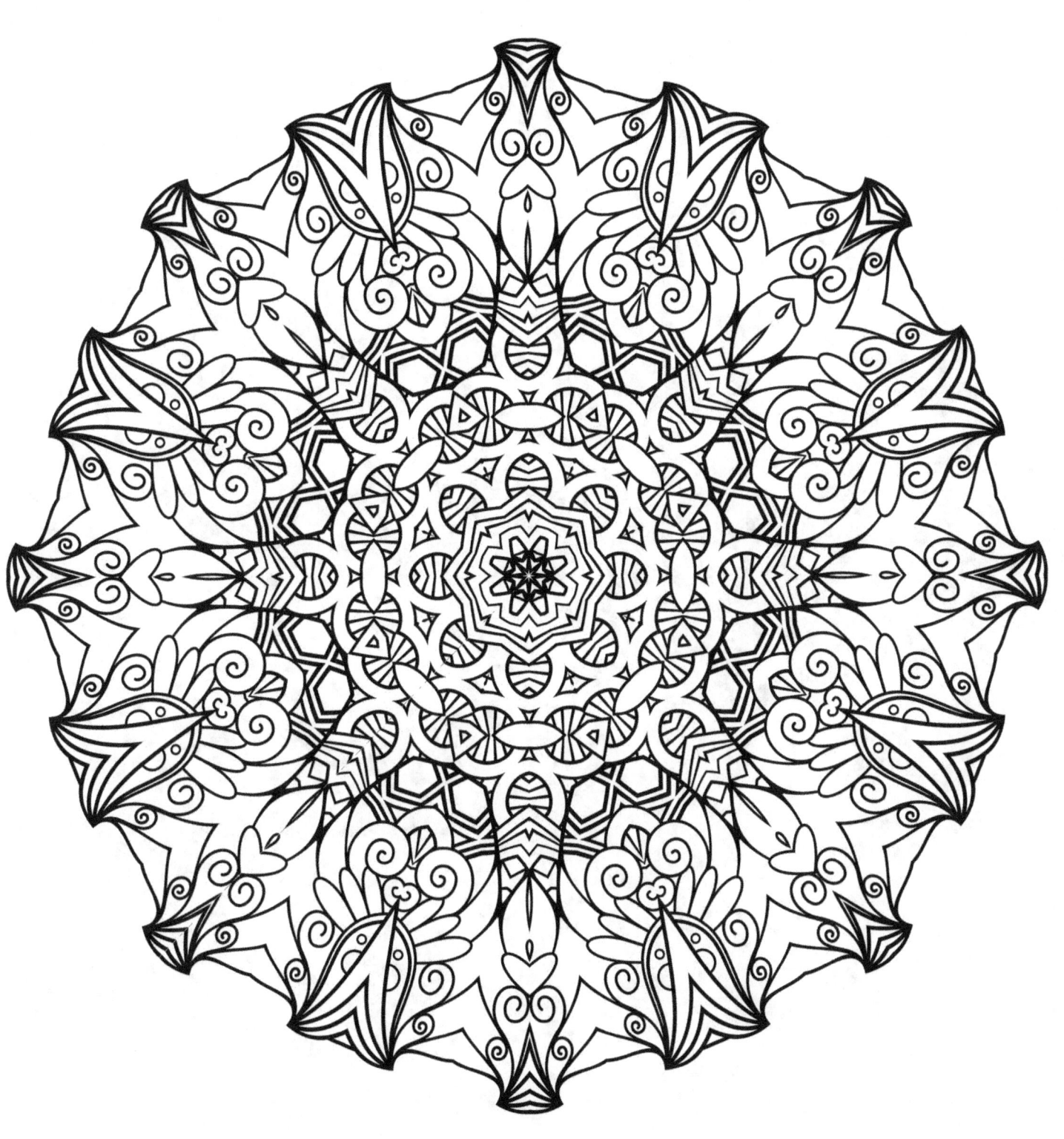

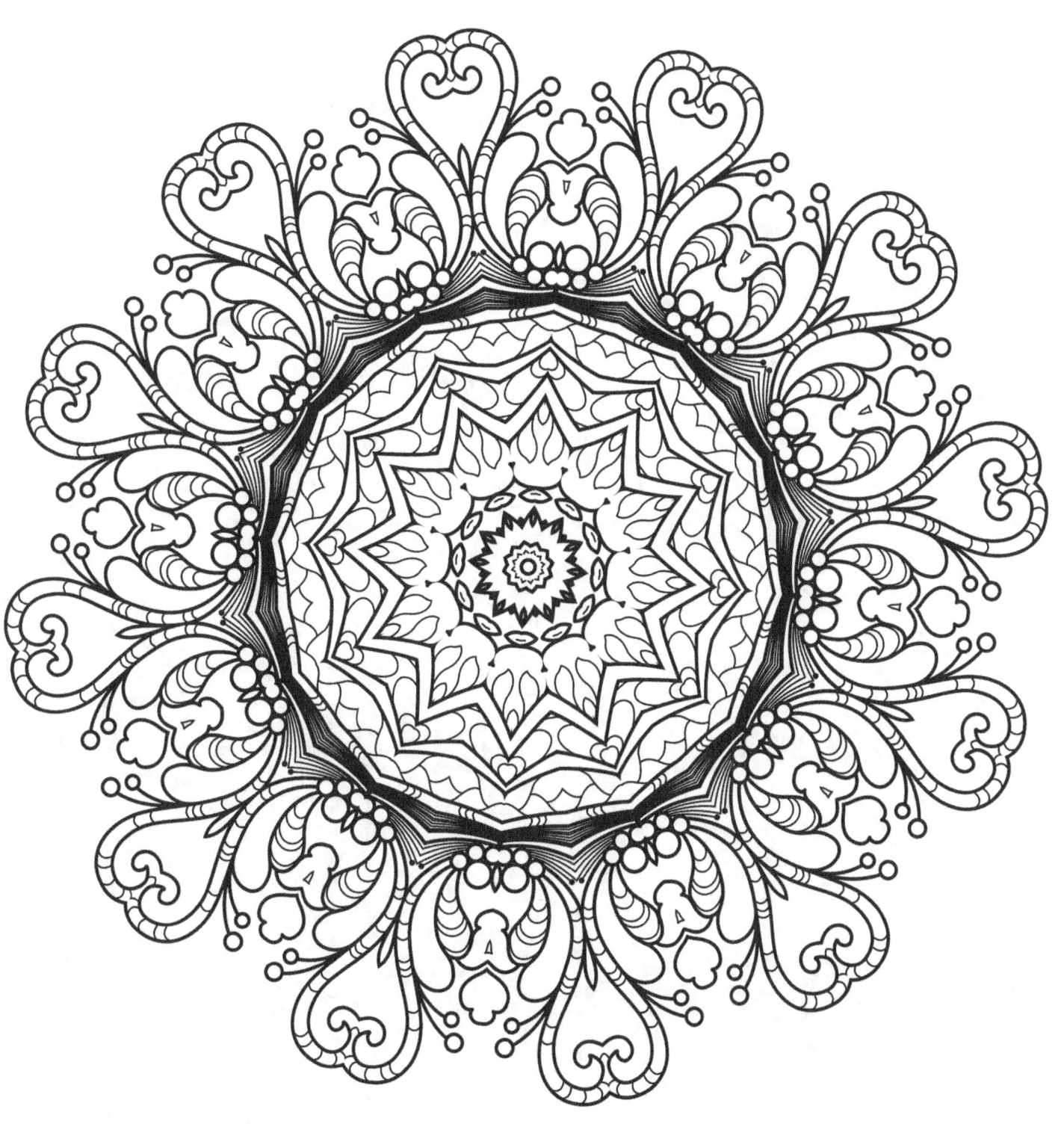

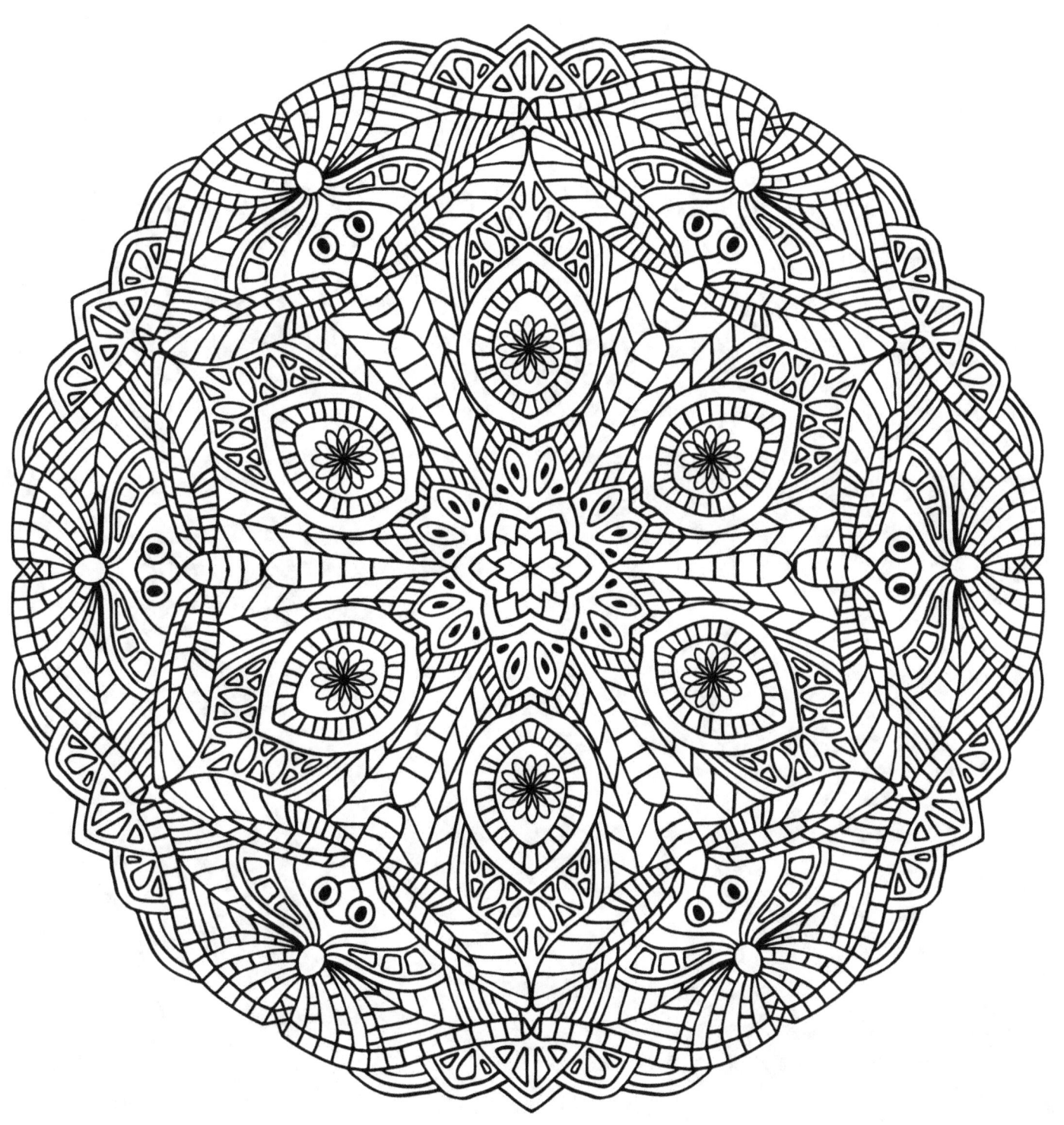

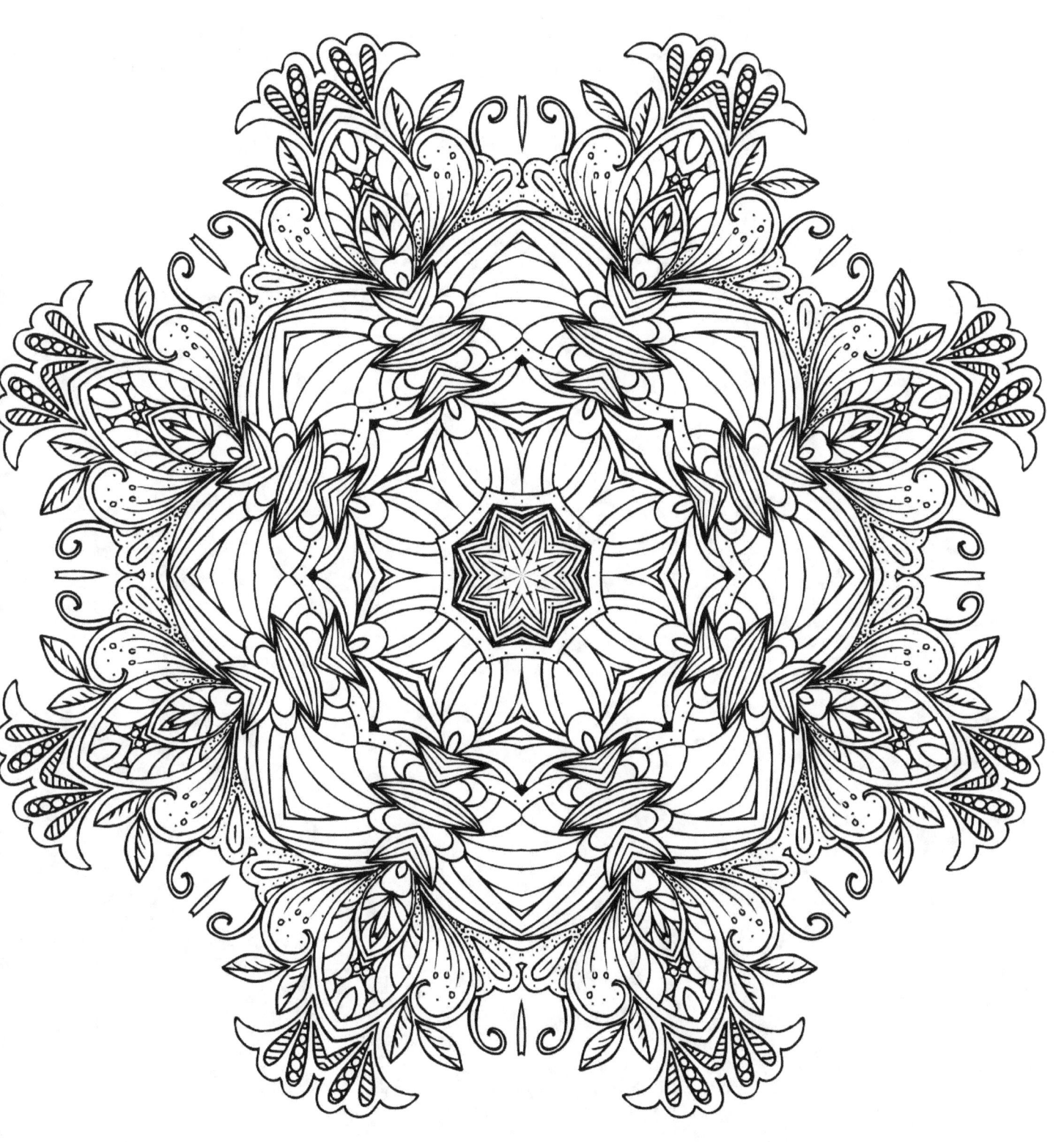

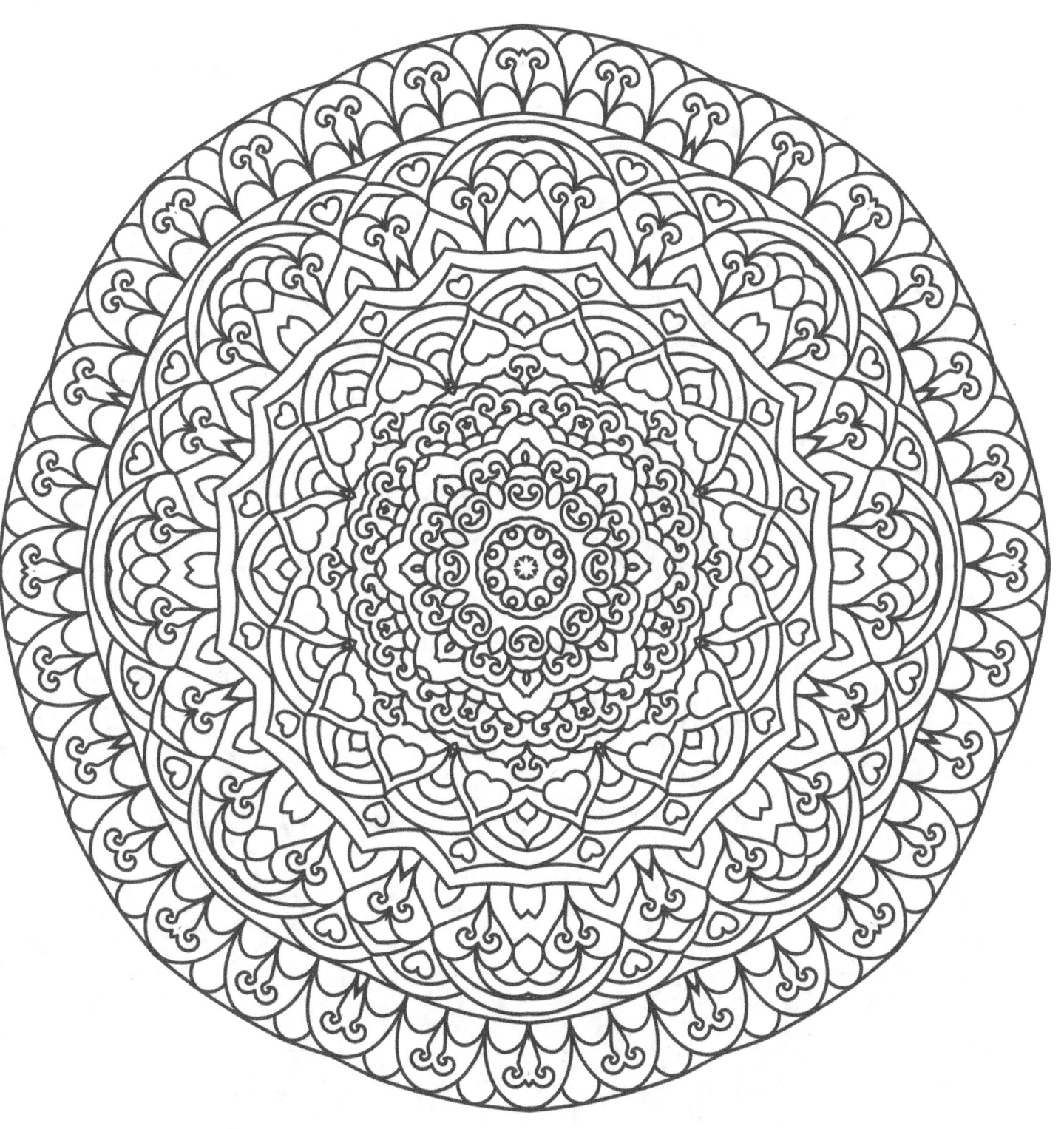

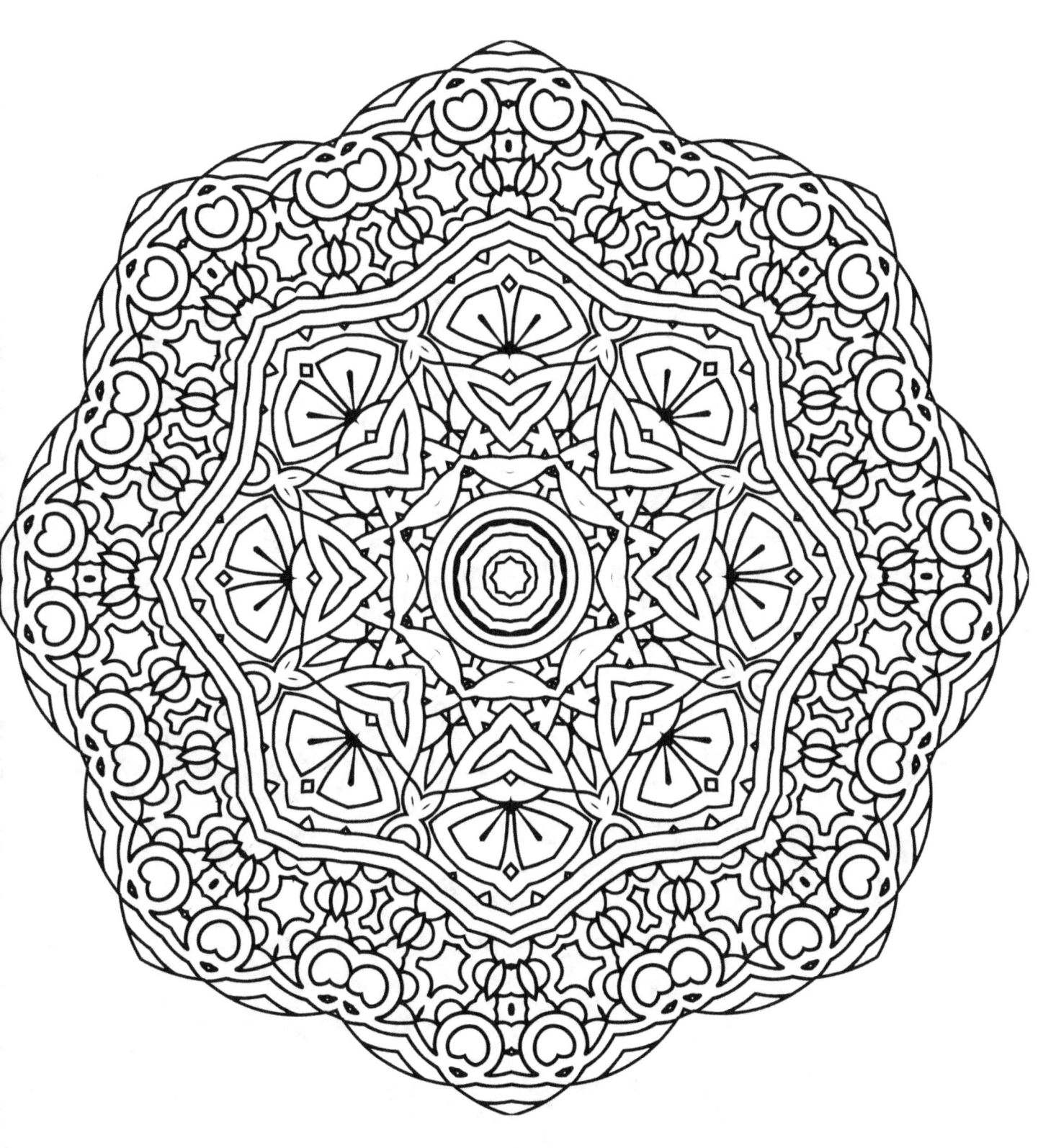

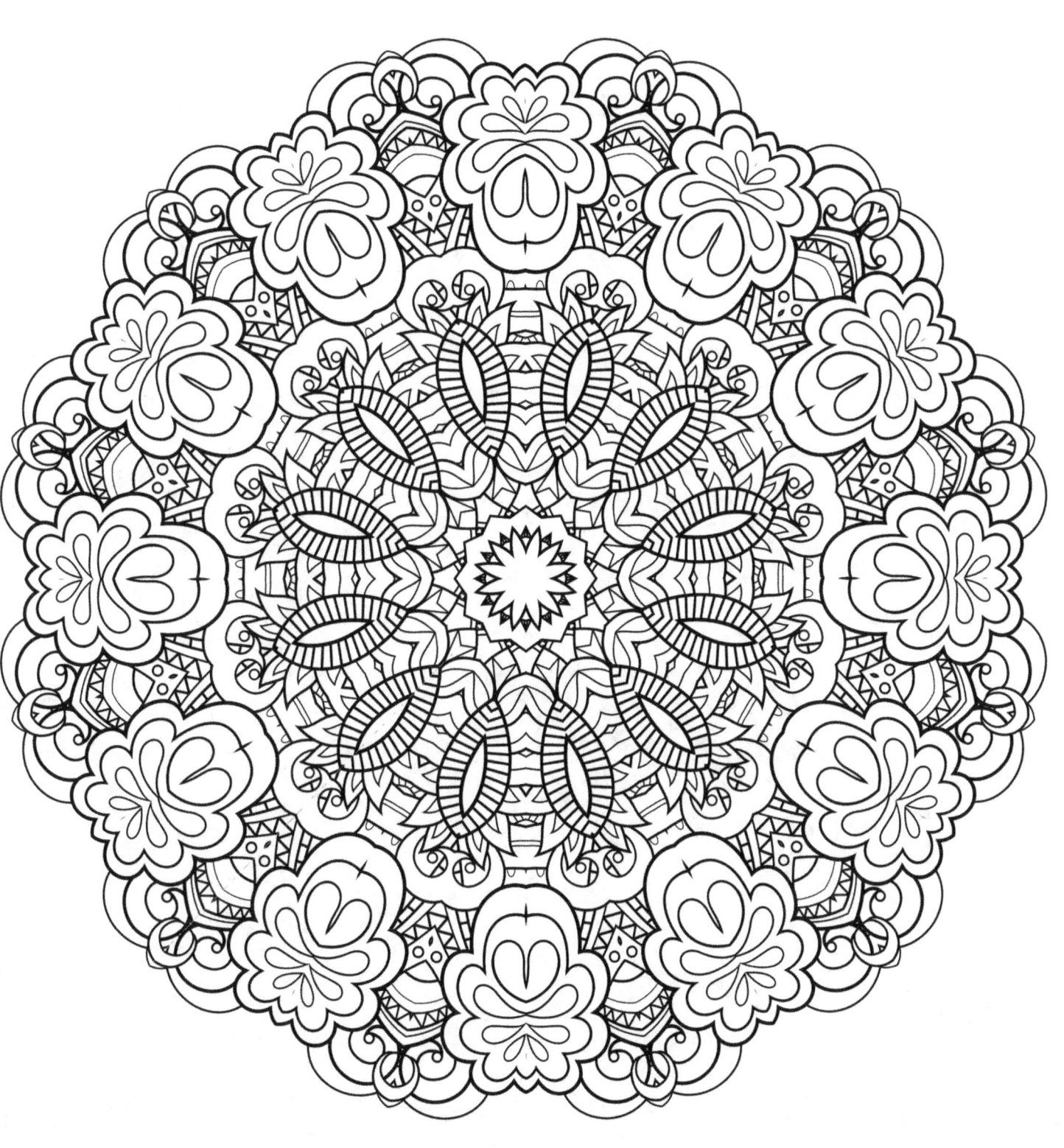

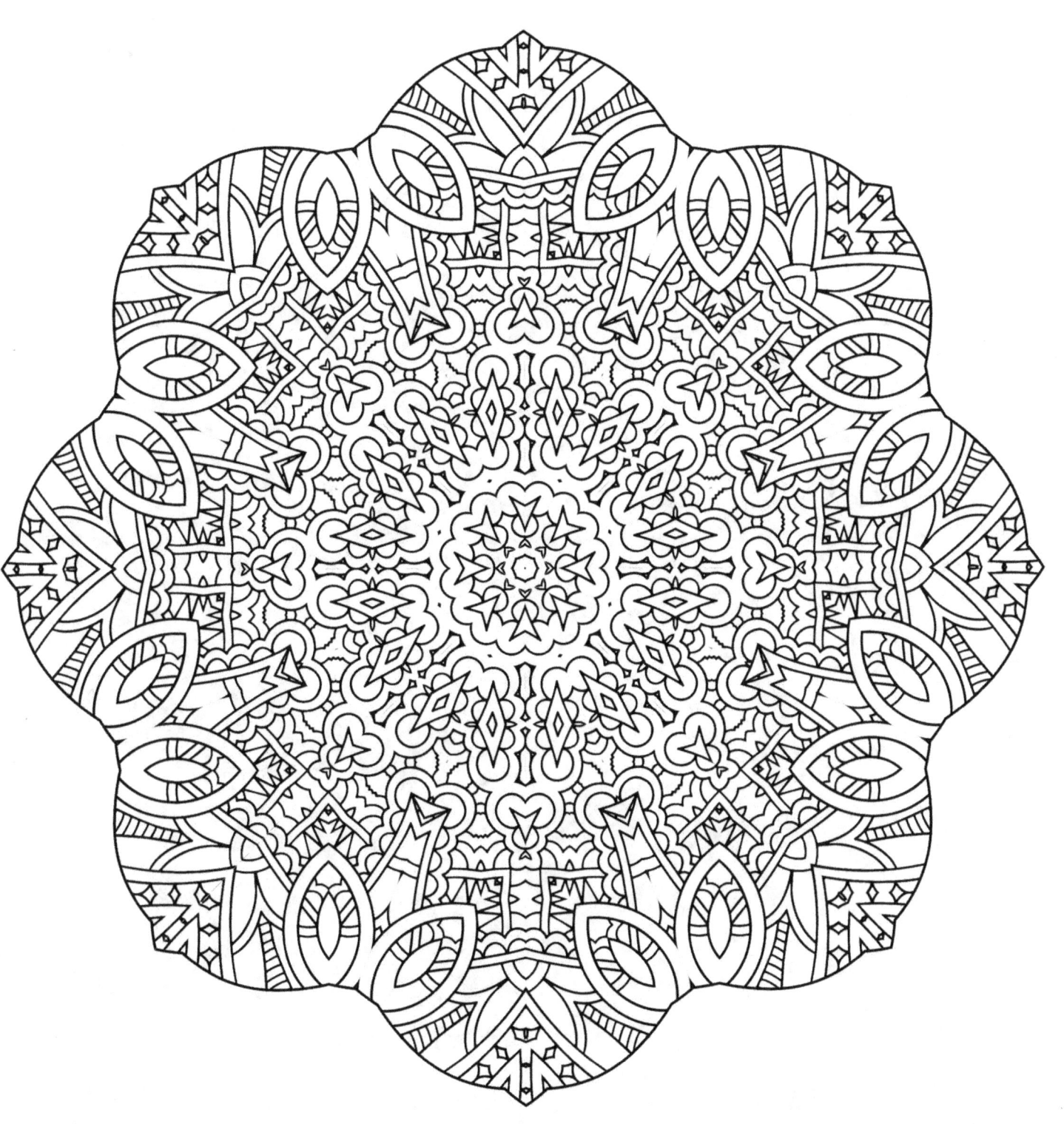

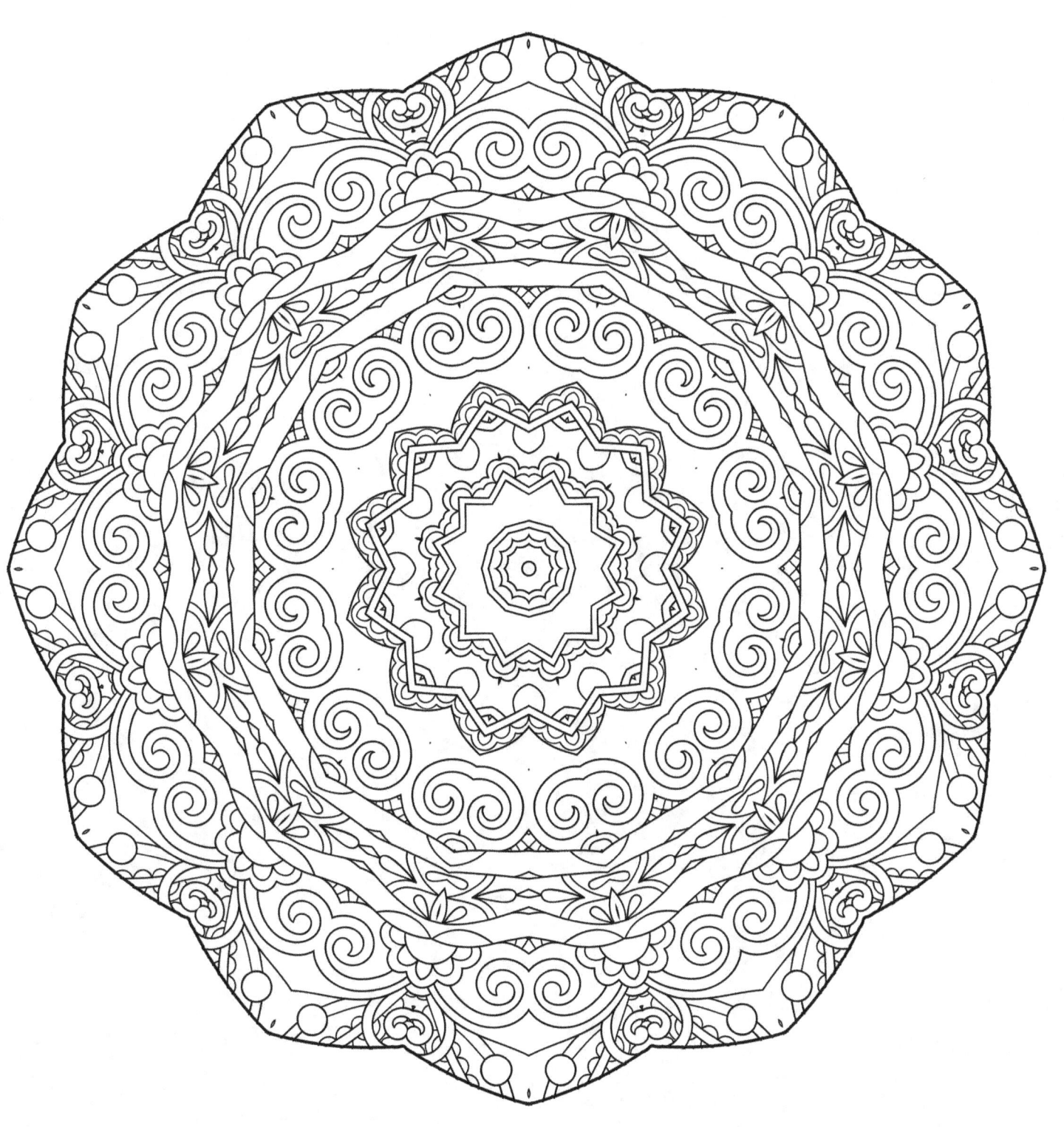

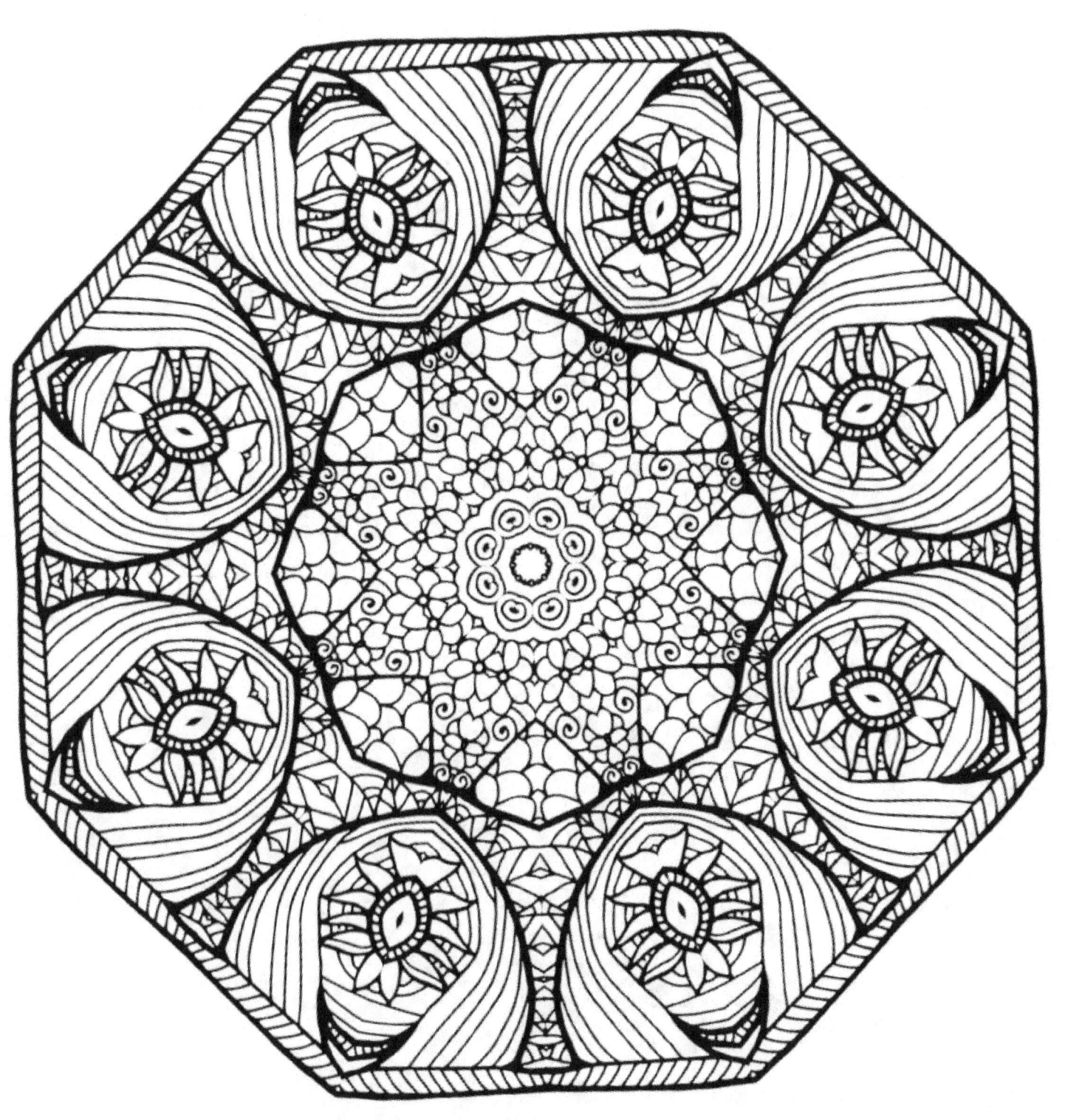

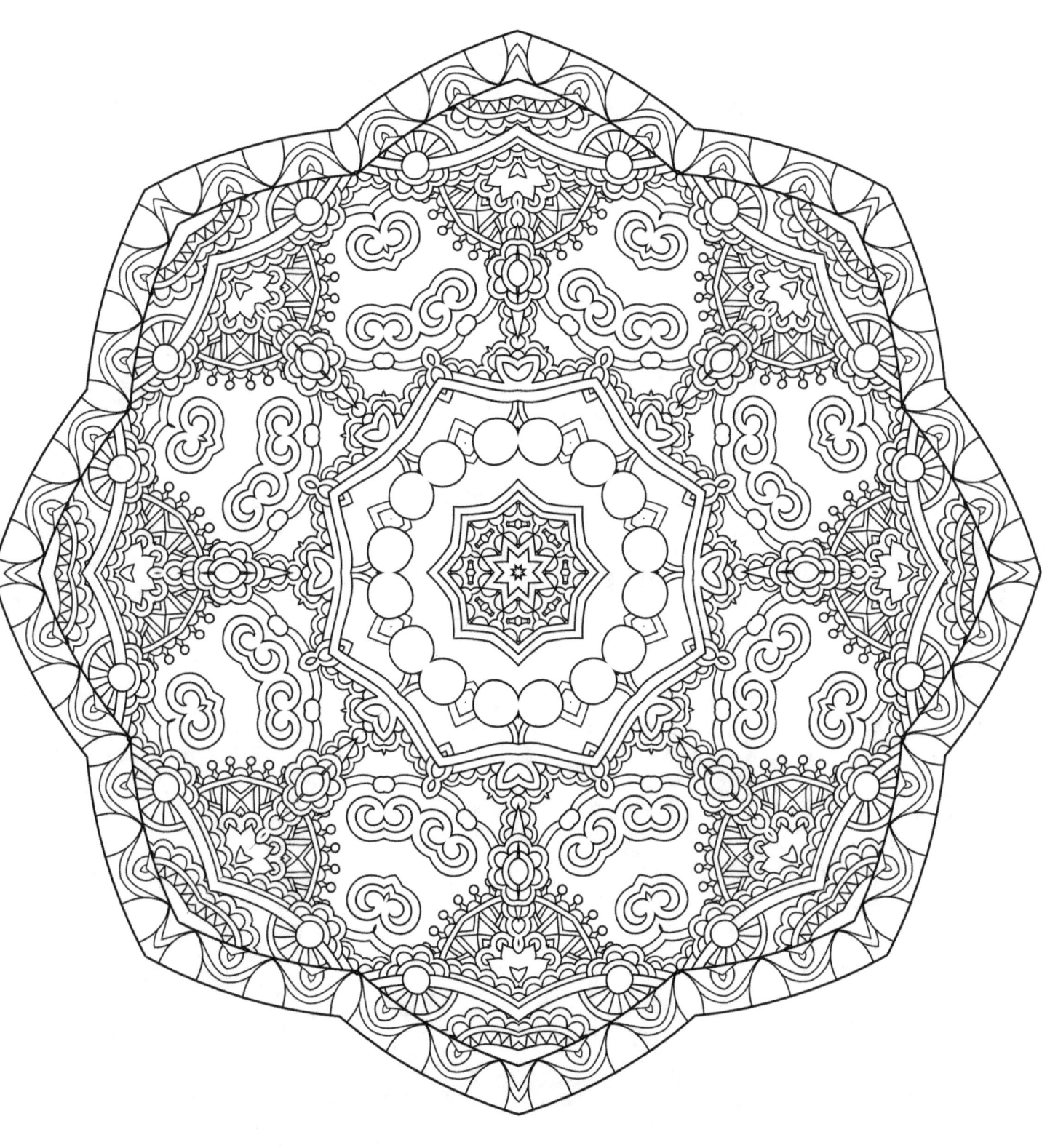

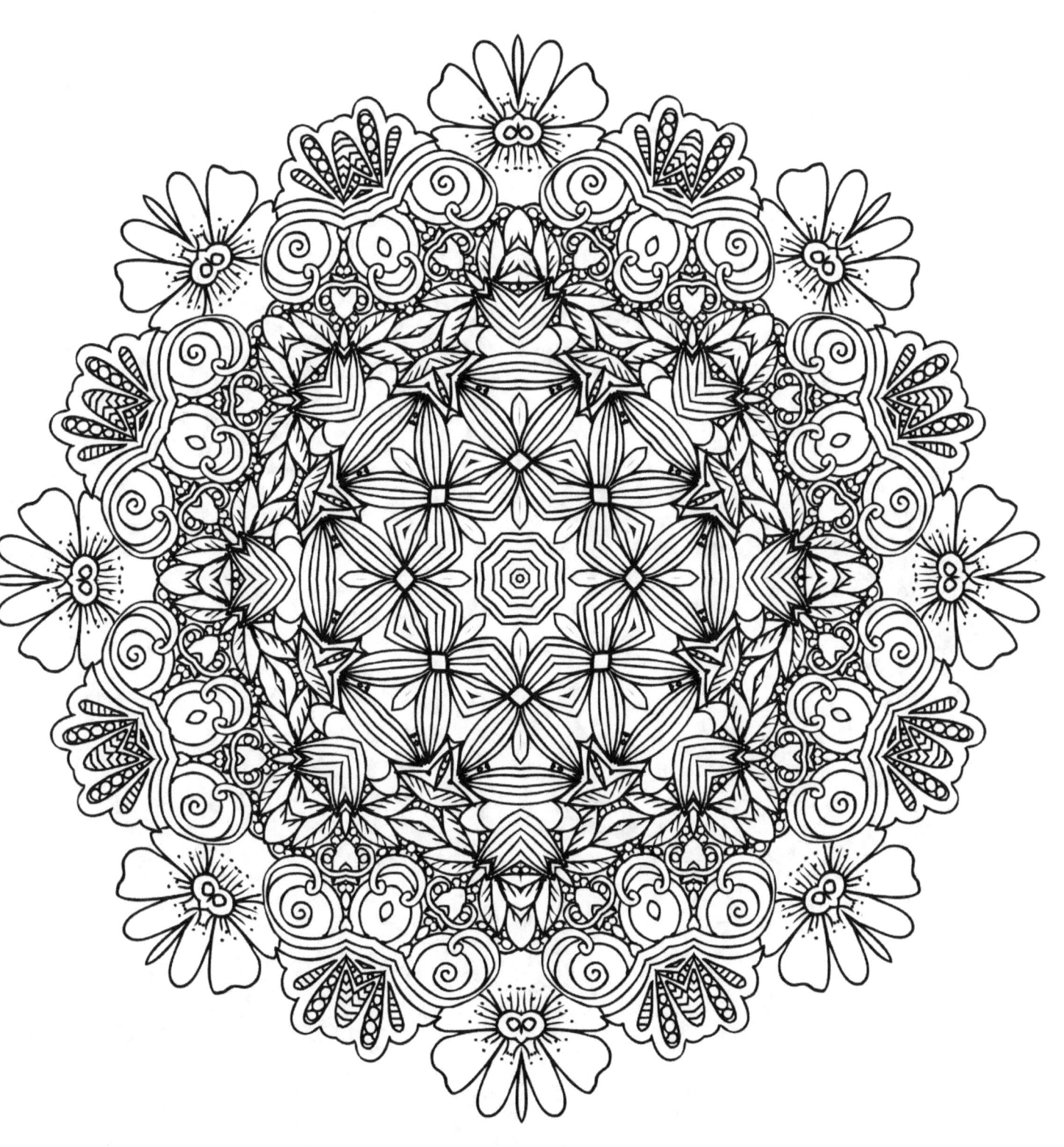

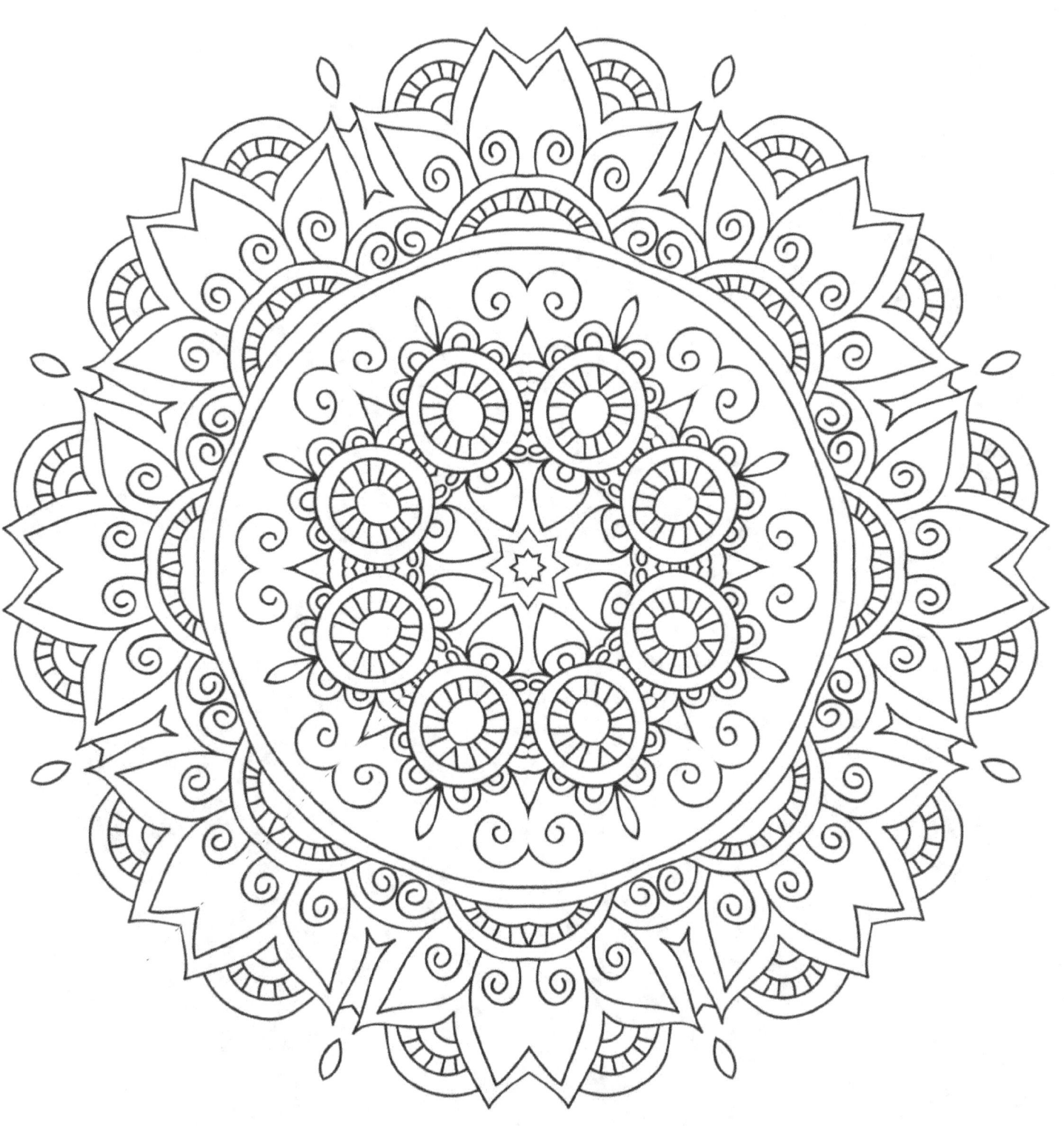

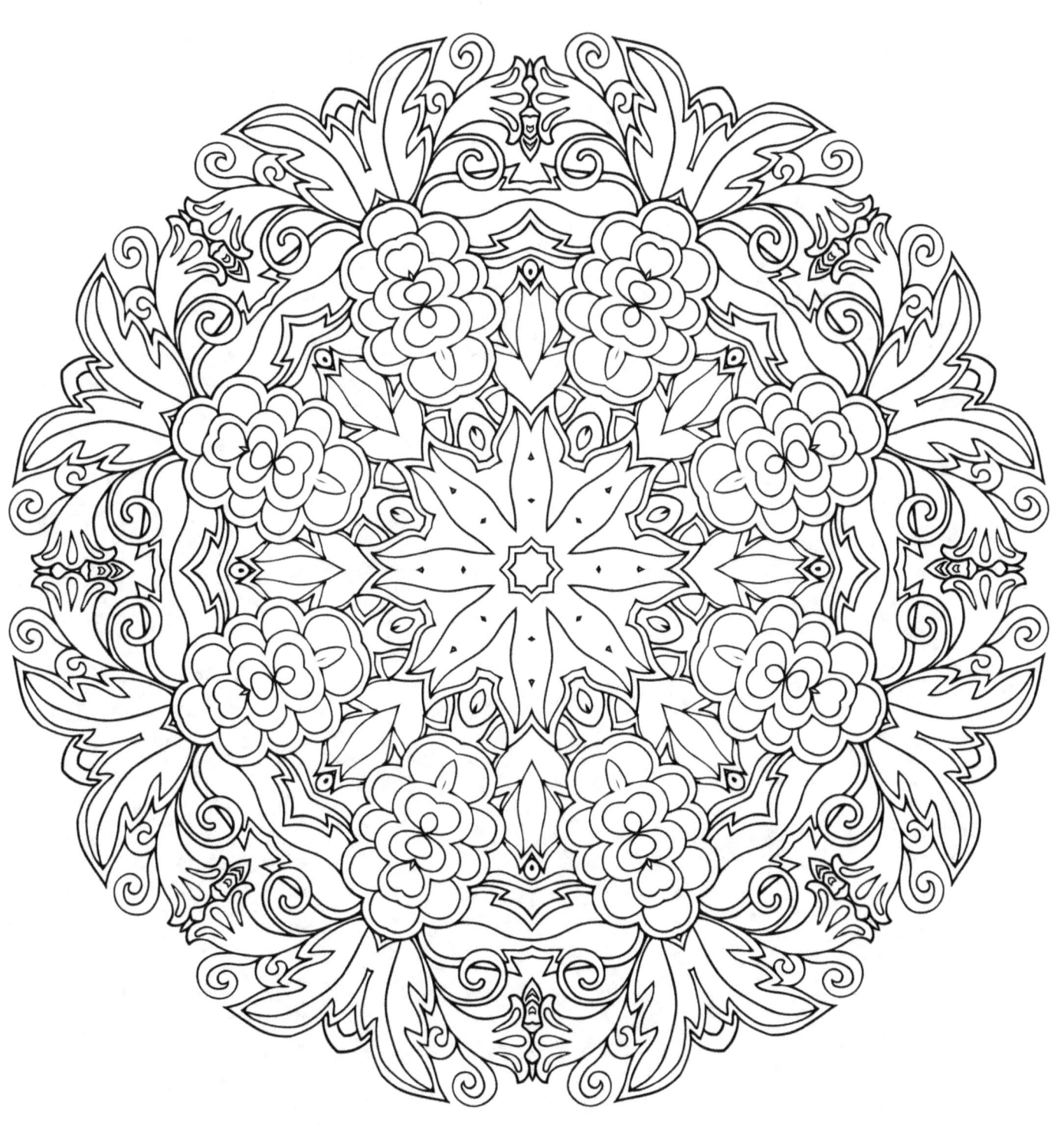

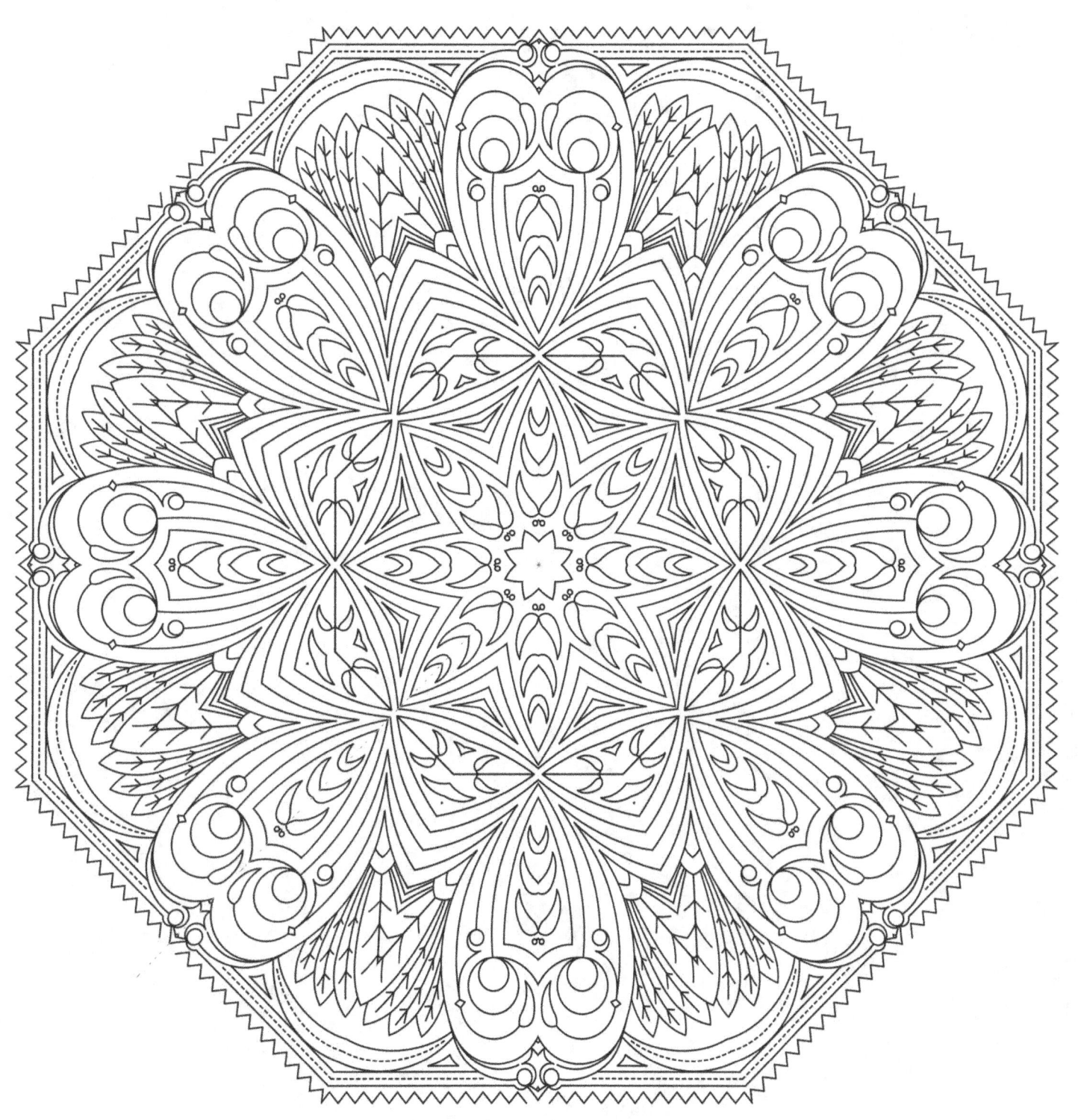

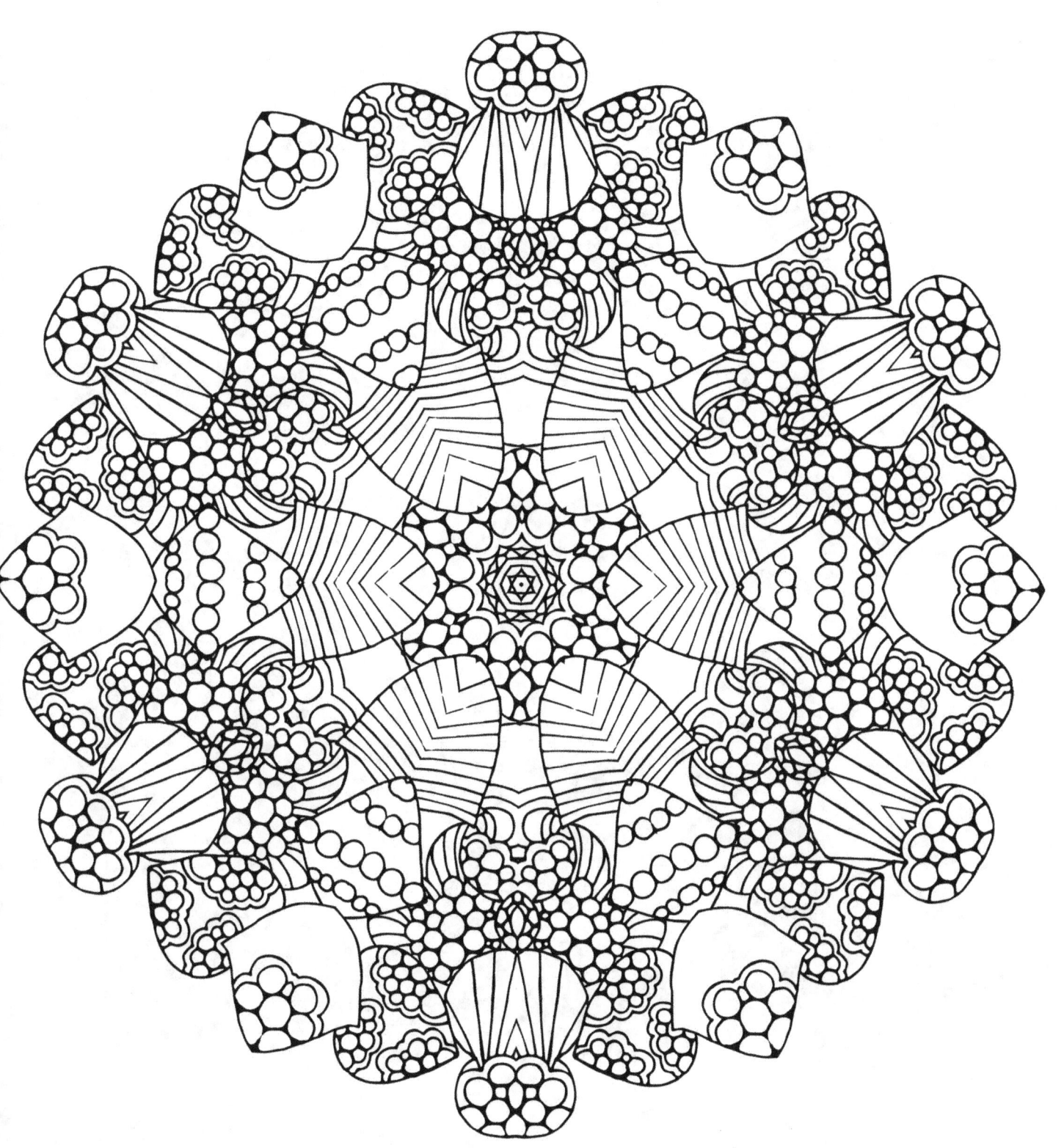

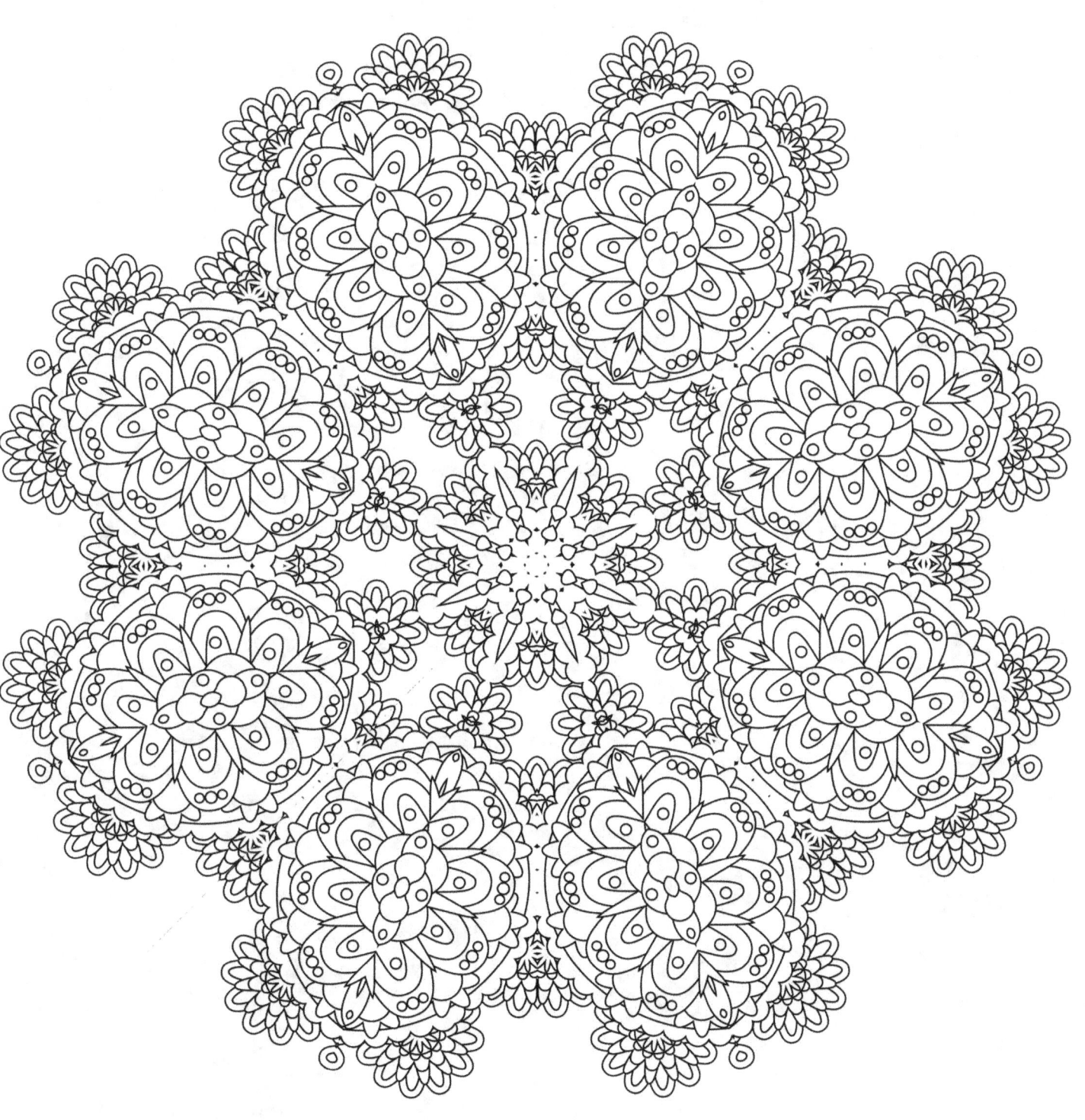

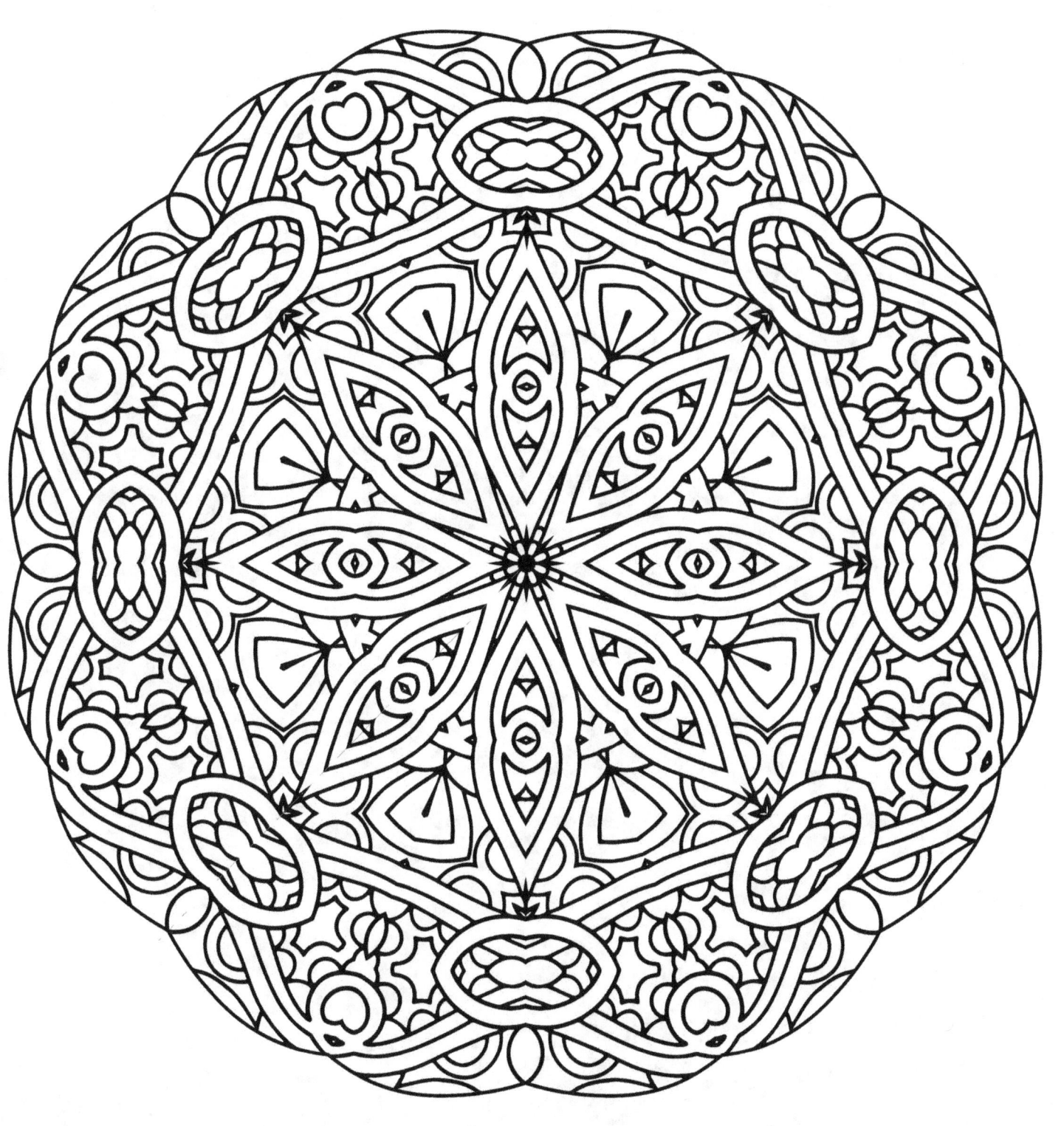

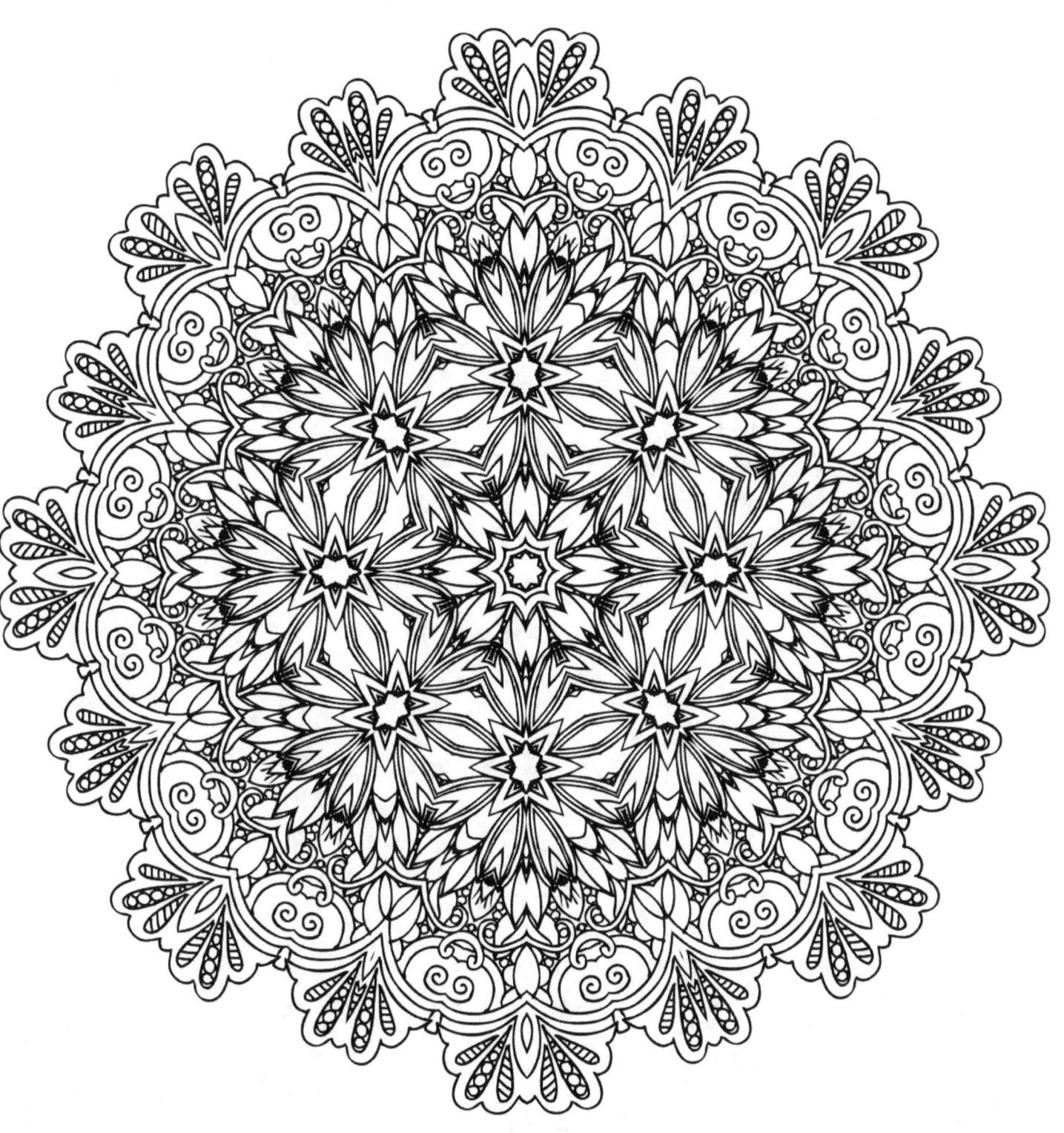

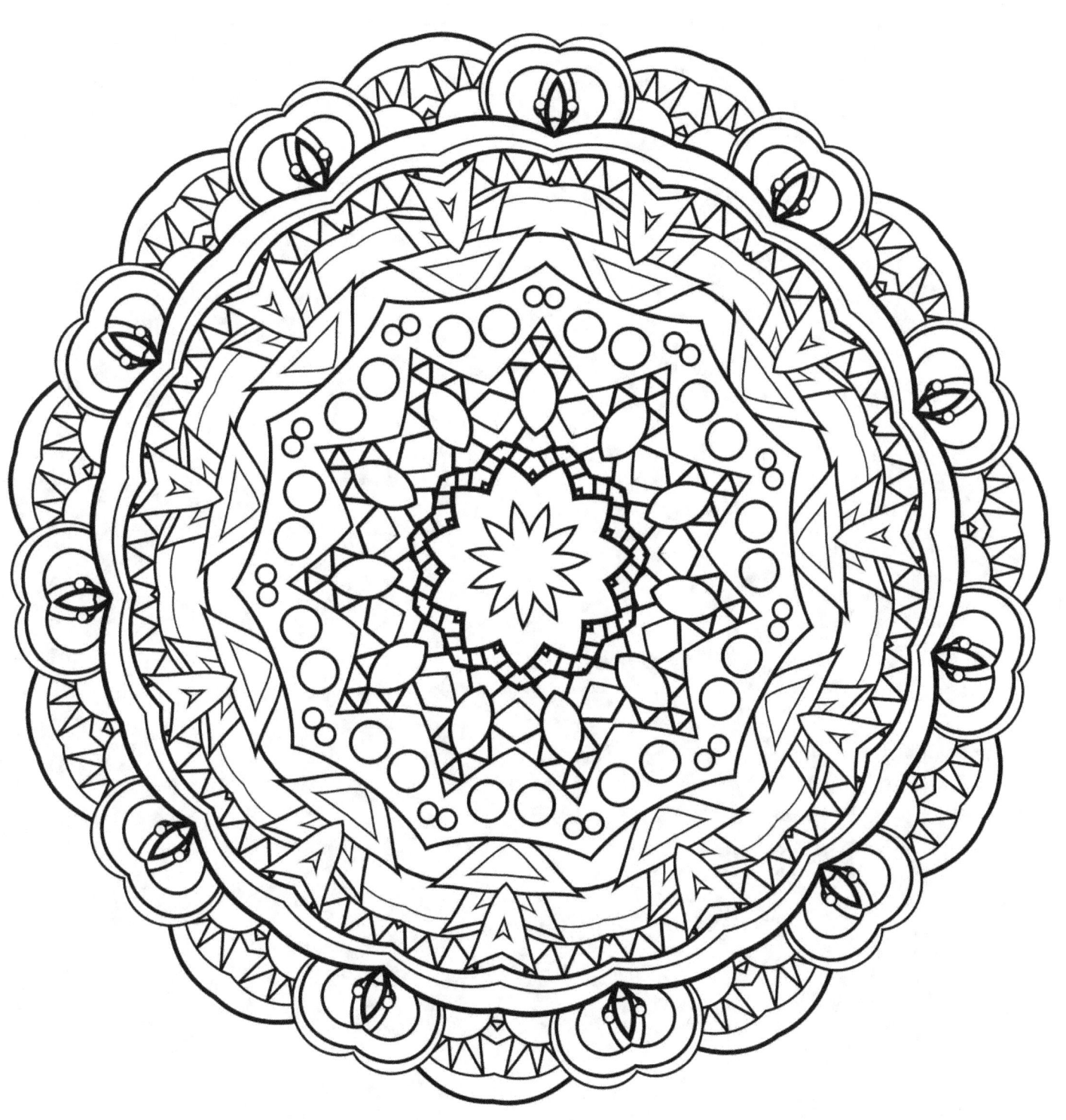

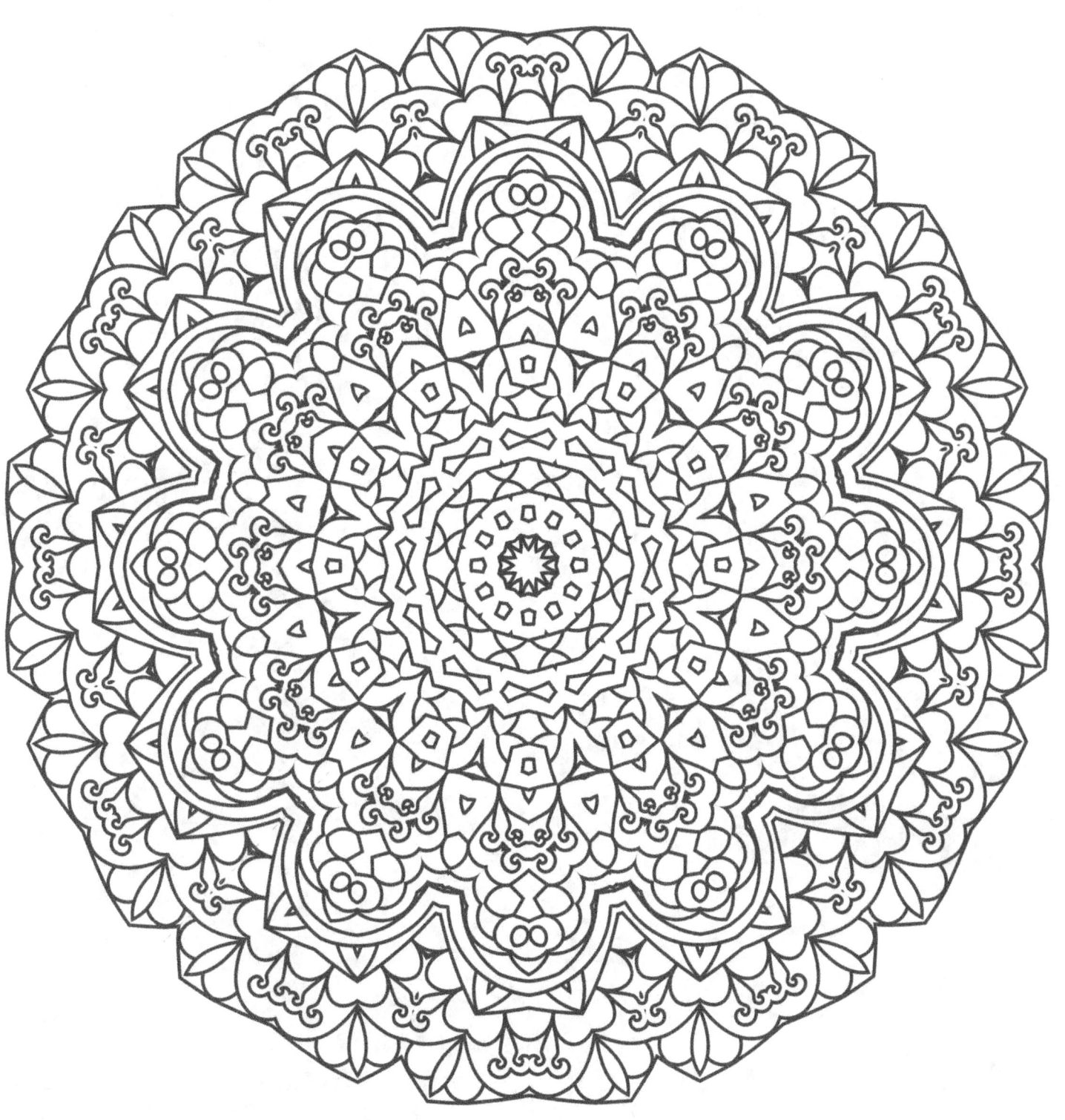

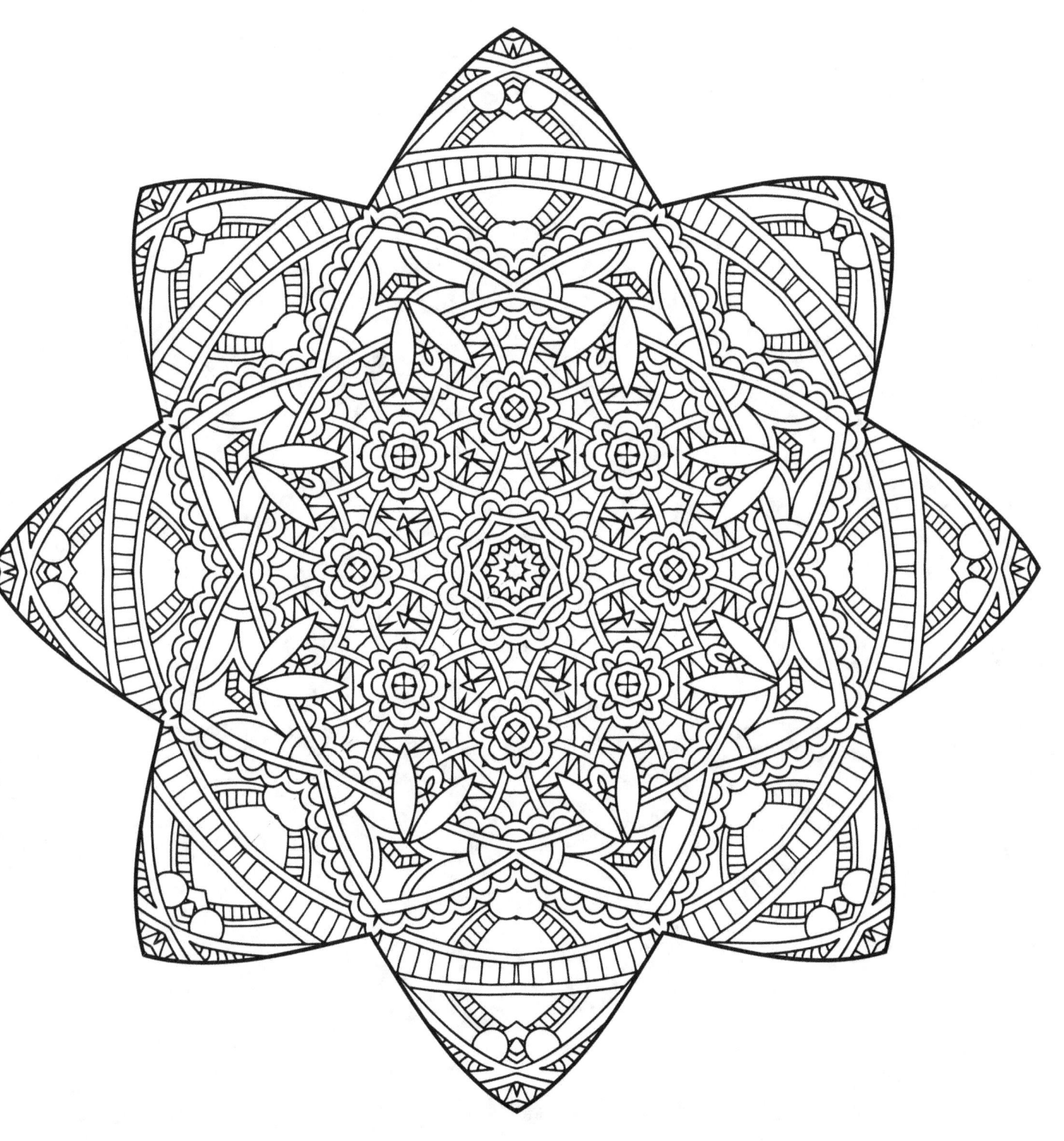

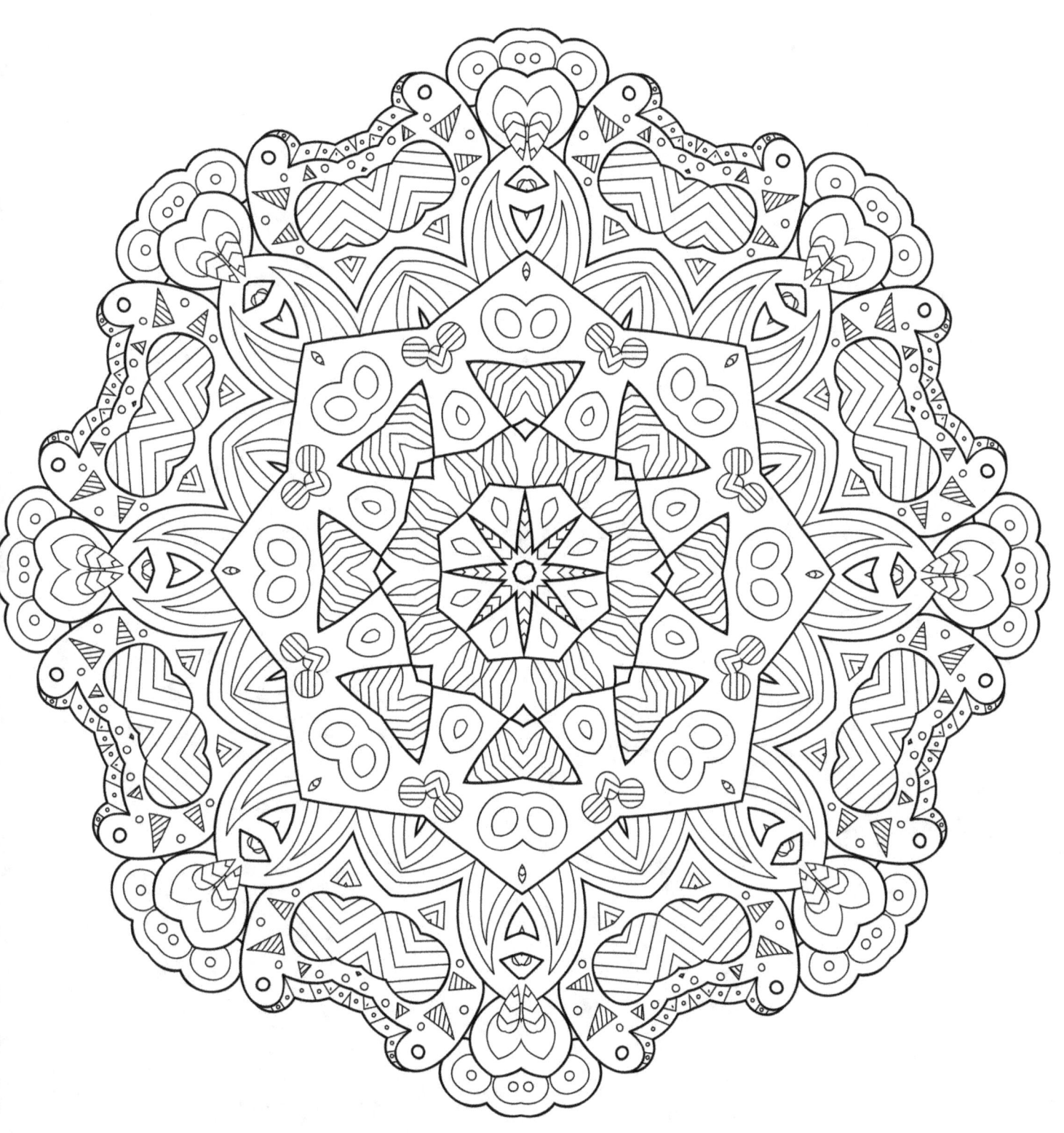

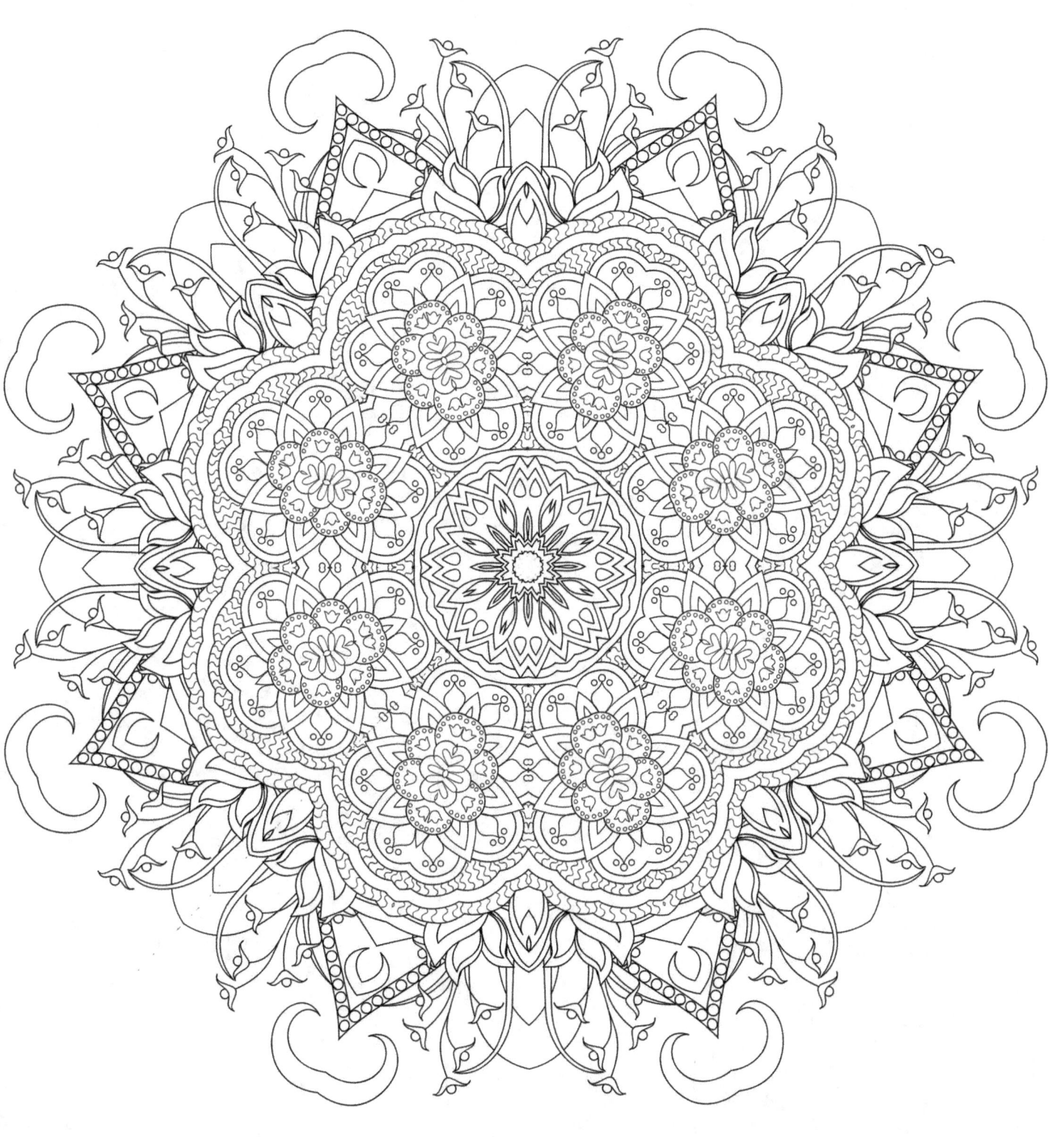

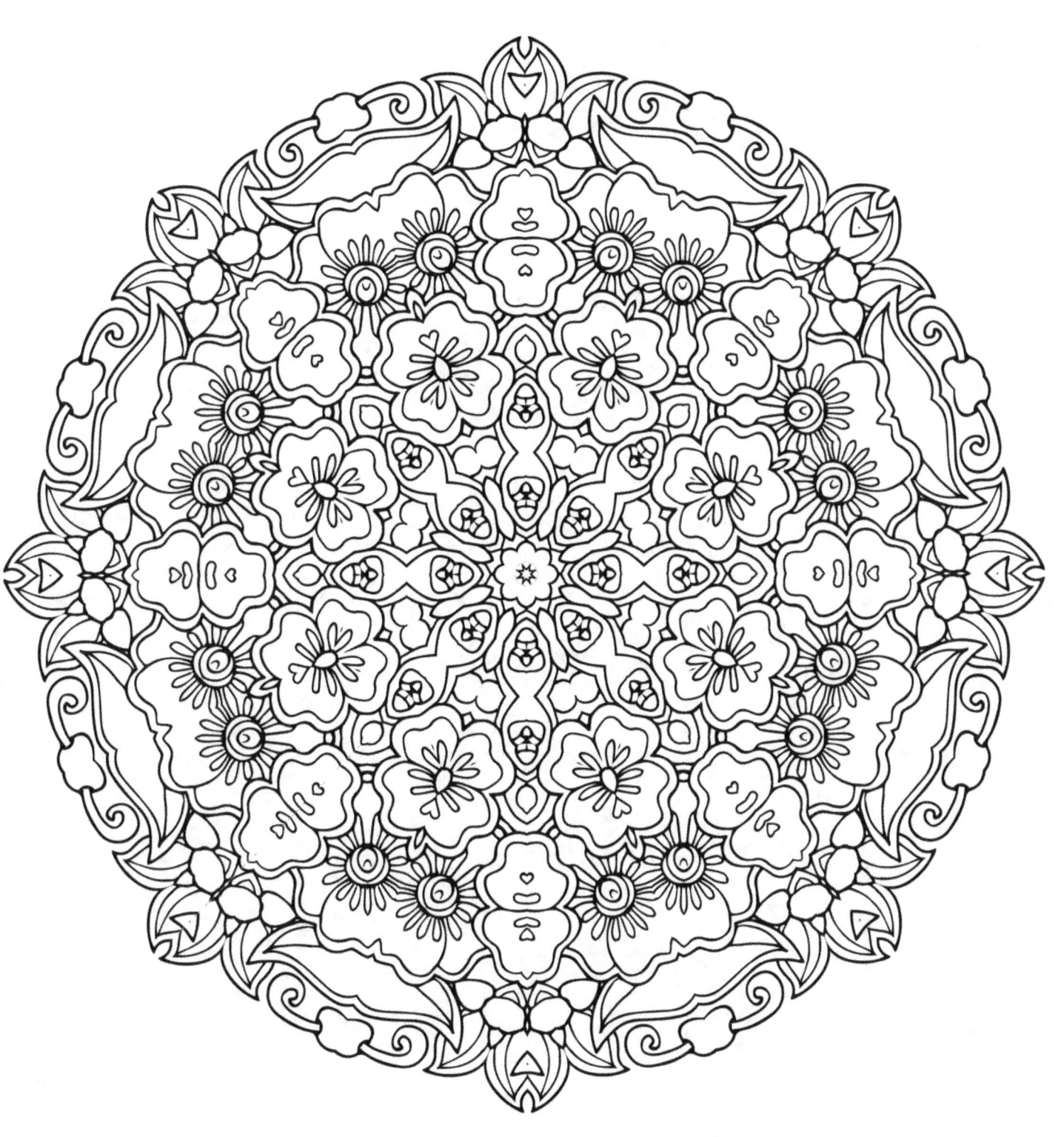

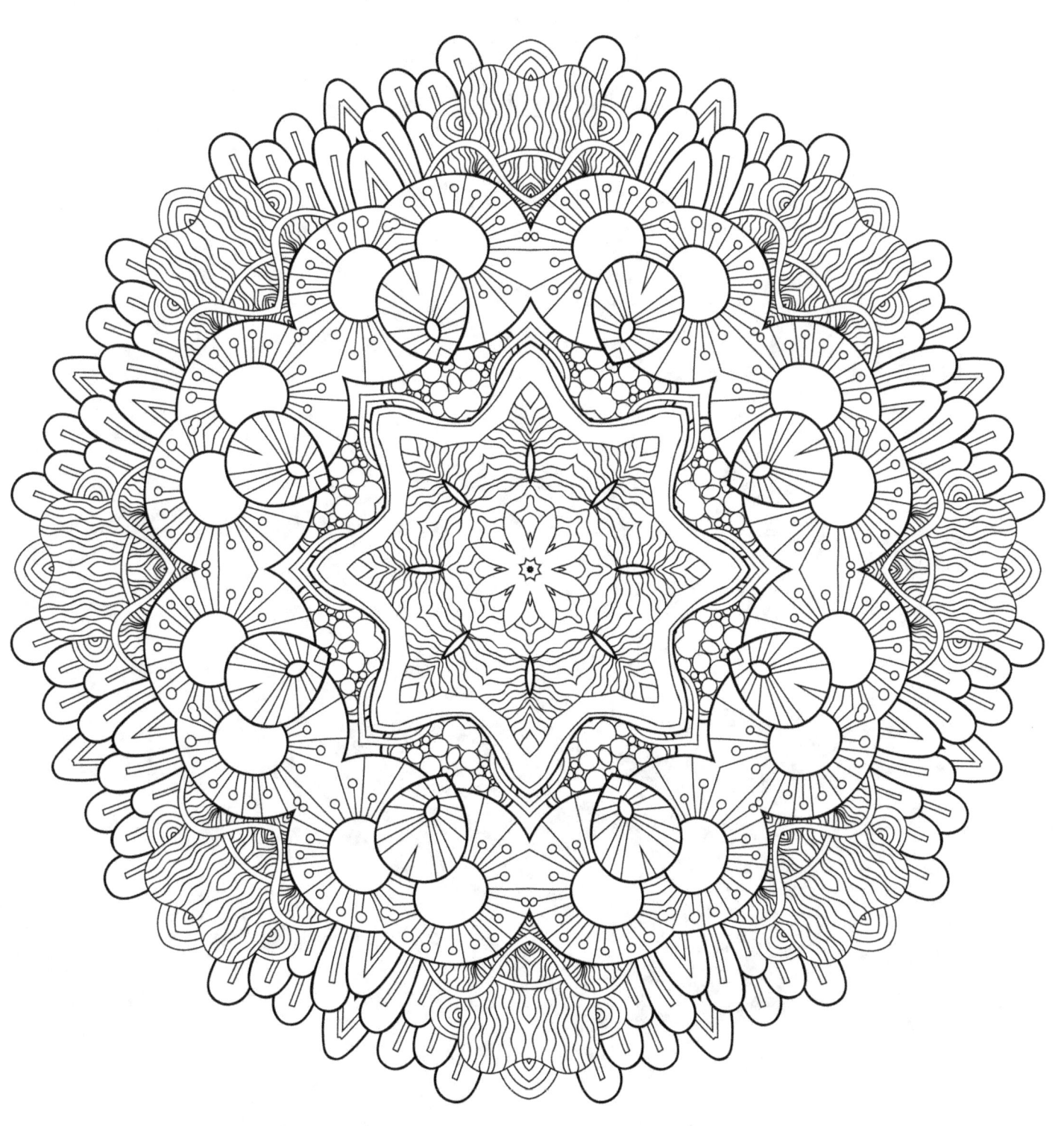

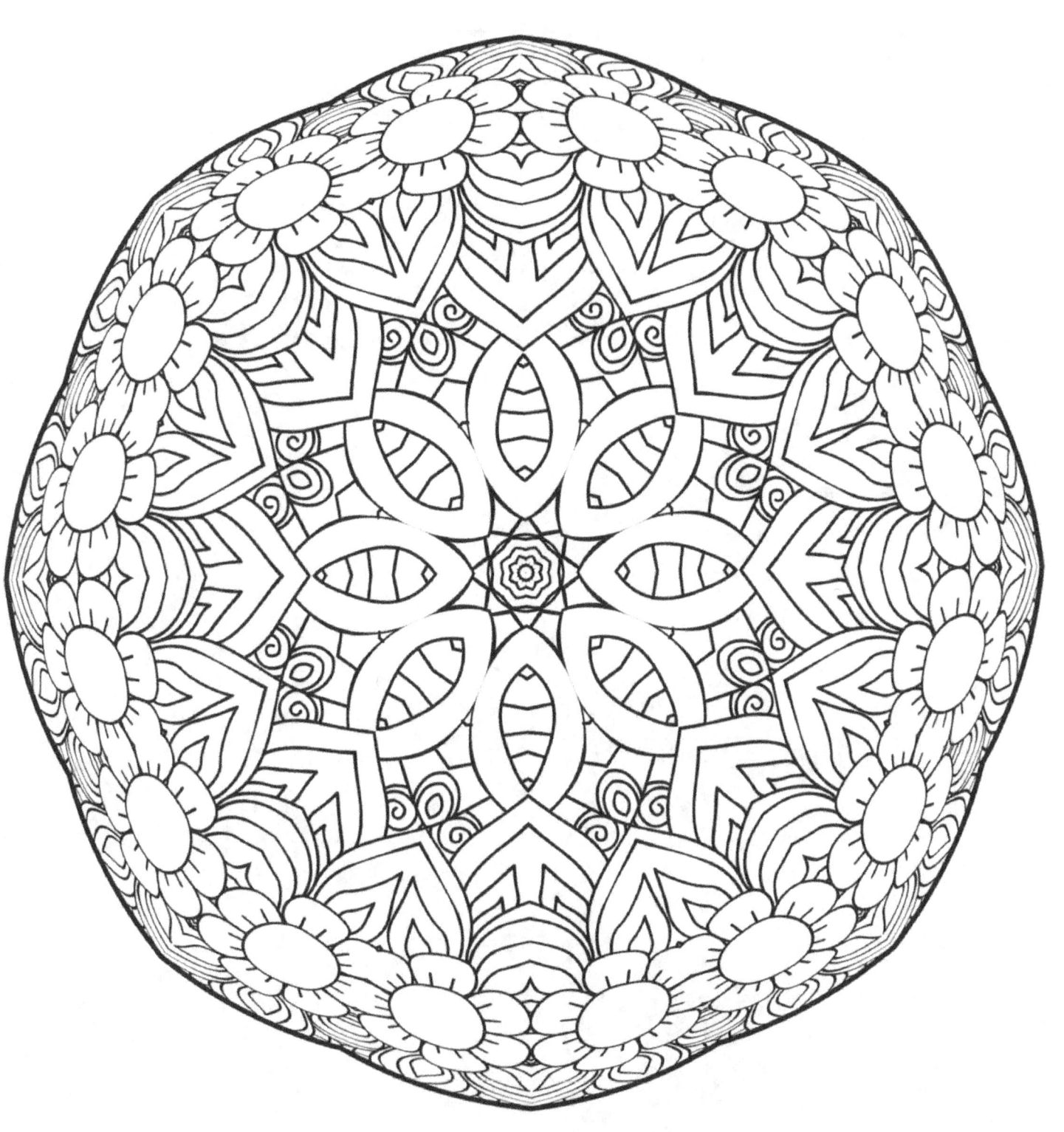

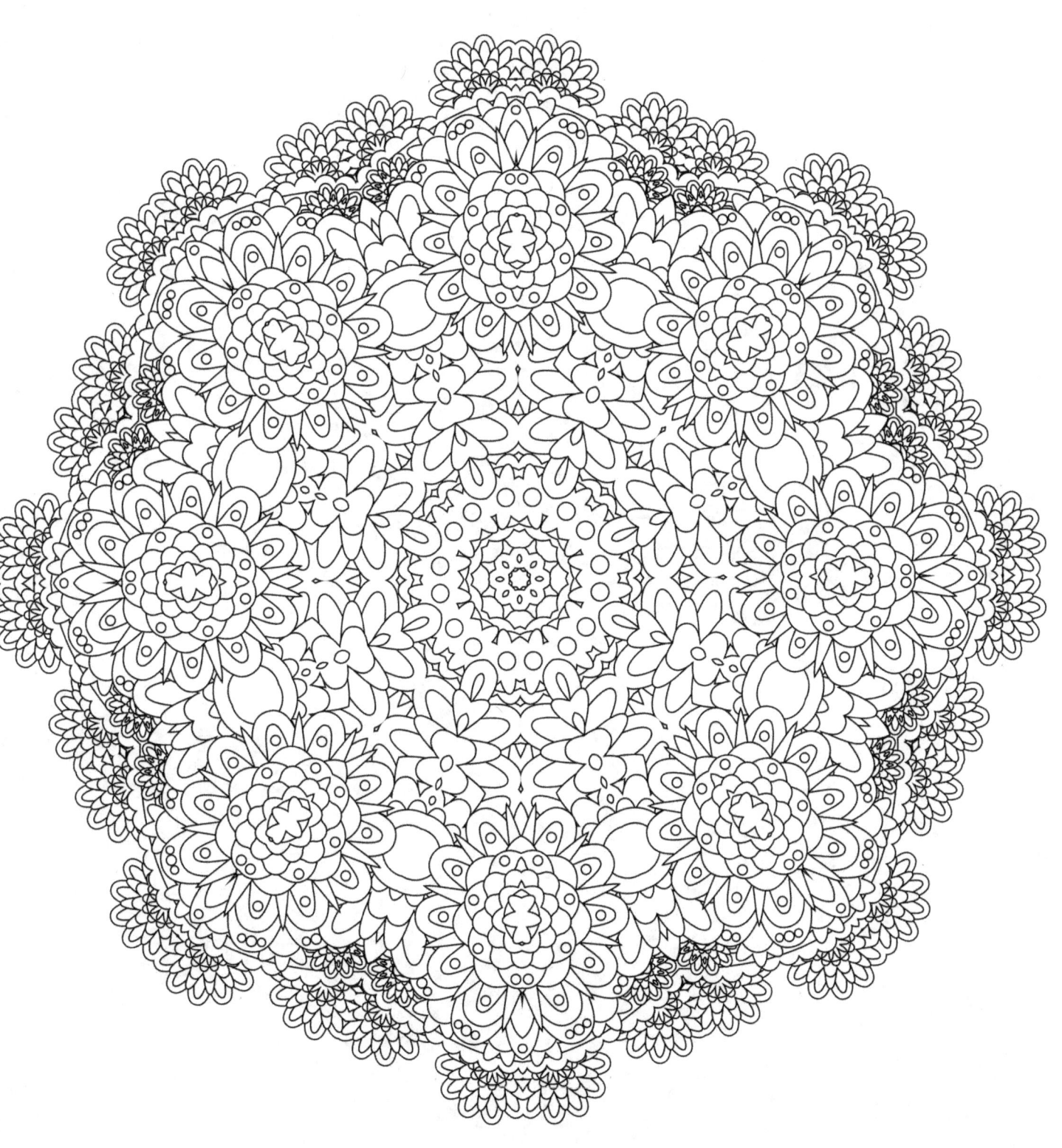

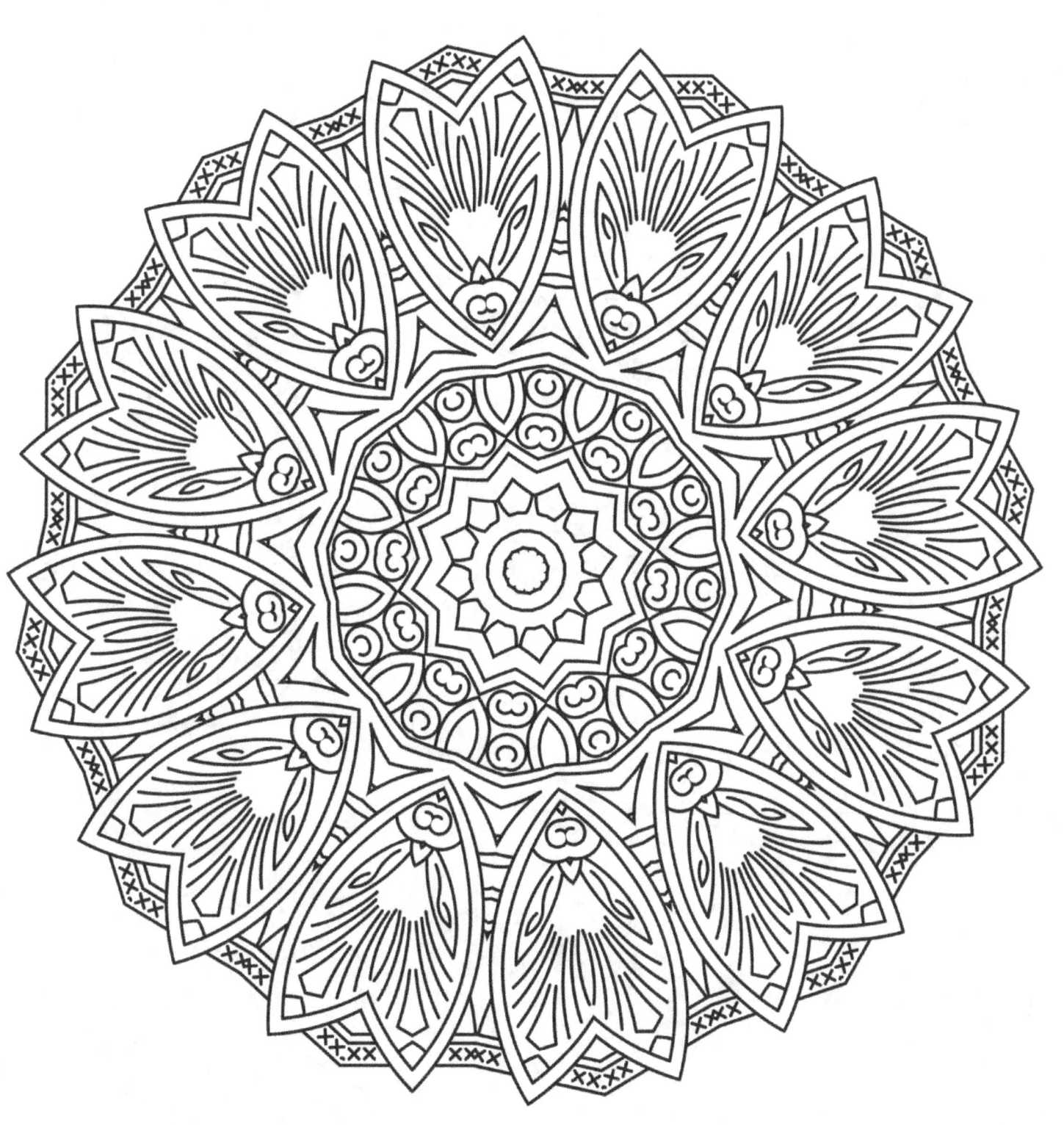

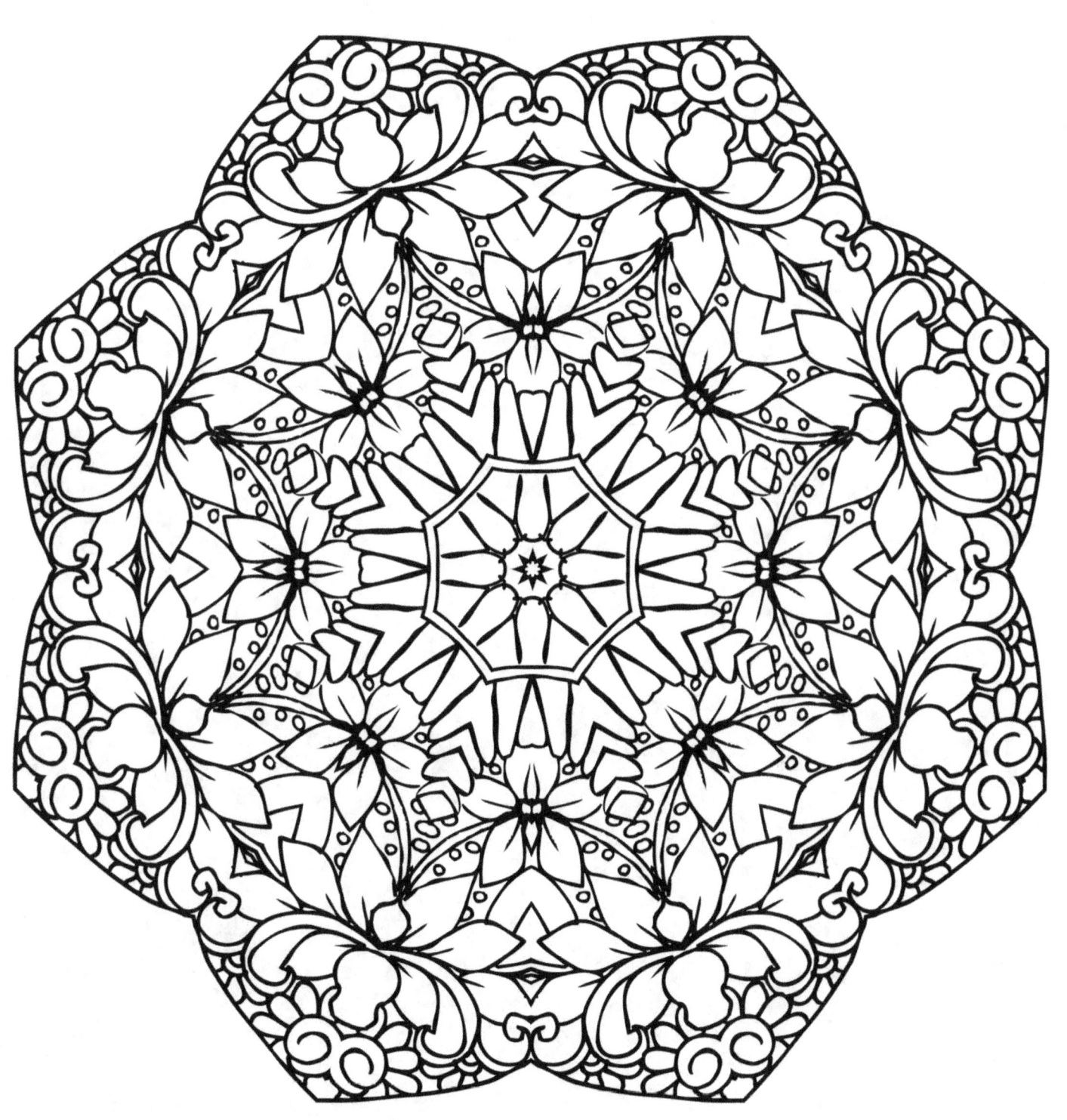

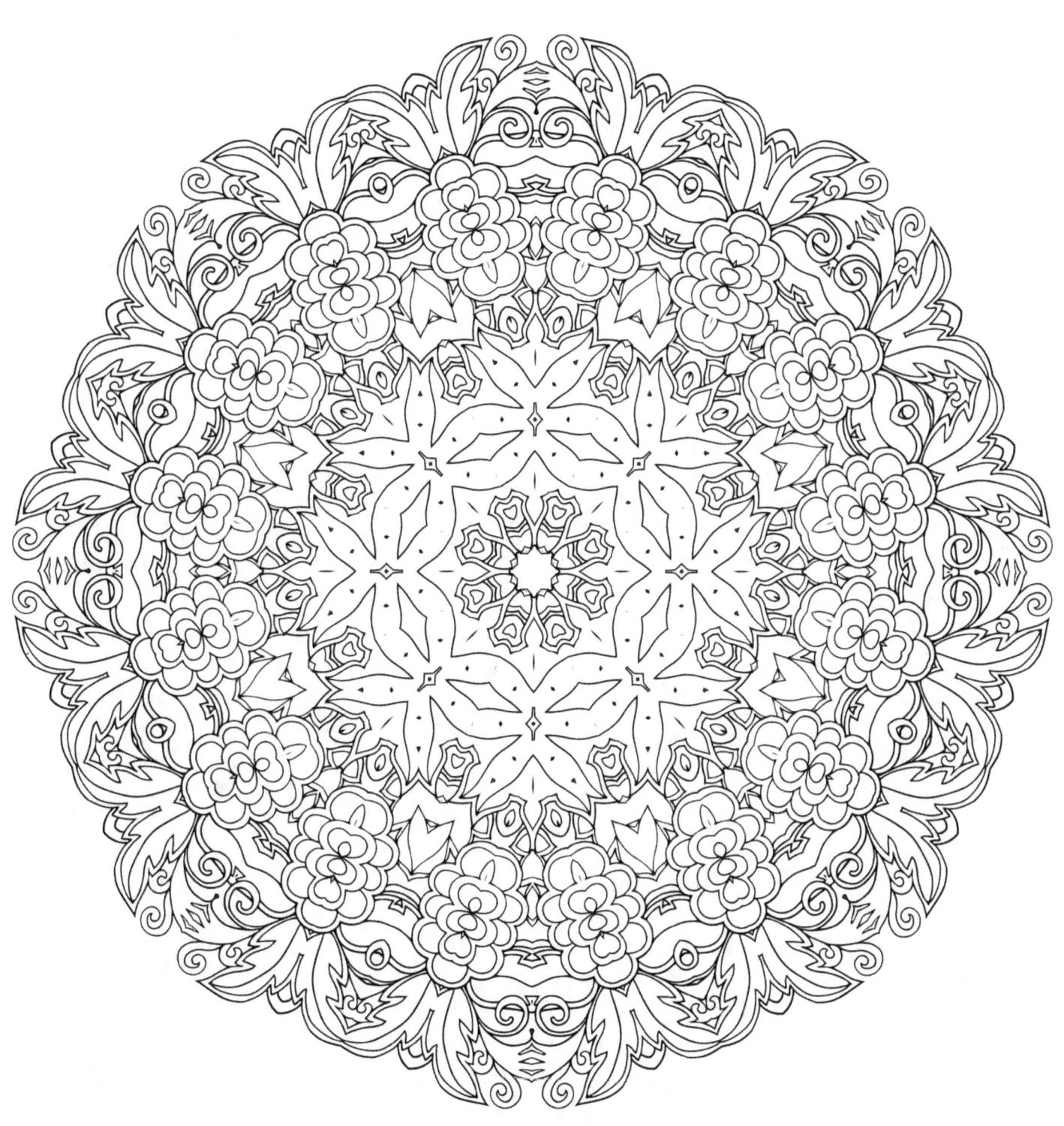